RESOURCE BOOKS FOR TEACHERS

series editor
ALAN MALEY

LEARNER-BASED TEACHING

Colin Campbell &
Hanna Kryszewska

D1377271

Oxford University Press

Oxford University Press
Walton Street, Oxford OX2 6DP

Oxford   New York   Toronto   Madrid
Delhi   Bombay   Calcutta   Madras   Karachi
Kuala Lumpur   Singapore   Hong Kong   Tokyo
Nairobi   Dar es Salaam   Cape Town
Melbourne   Auckland

and associated companies in
Berlin   Ibadan

Oxford and *Oxford English* are trade marks of
Oxford University Press

ISBN 0 19 437163 8

© Oxford University Press 1992

First published 1992
Second impression 1993

All rights reserved. No part of this publication may be
reproduced, stored in a retrieval system, or transmitted, in any
form or by any means, electronic, mechanical, photocopying,
recording, or otherwise, without the prior permission of
Oxford University Press.

This book is sold subject to the condition that it shall not, by
way of trade or otherwise, be lent, re-sold, hired out, or
otherwise circulated without the publisher's prior consent in
any form of binding or cover other than that in which it is
published and without a similar condition including this
condition being imposed on the subsequent purchaser.

Set by Wyvern Typesetting Ltd

Printed in Hong Kong

Acknowledgements

We would like to thank the people from whom we have learned so much: all our students and colleagues everywhere, but especially those at the English Language Centre at the University of Gdansk who willingly participated in the activities and tried out the ideas and who allowed us to include their materials as sample products; and teacher trainers we have met, both in the United Kingdom and in Poland, and the authors of books from which we have also learned. We owe a lot to the following people whose work has inspired us: Mario Rinvolucri, John Morgan, Chris Sion, Alan Maley, and Alan Duff, among others.

We also thank all of those who are dear to us for their support and encouragement.

Finally we would like to acknowledge how much we have learned from each other. Working together was a pleasure.

Hanna and Colin.

Contents

2 Vocabulary

3 Integrated skills

The authors and series editor

Colin Campbell began his career in EFL in 1976, and has worked in Spain, England, and Italy, where he prepared, with a friend, a series of 15-minute programmes teaching English on local television. He did his MA in Applied Linguistics at Reading University, and in 1984 moved to Poland to work as Director of Studies at the British Council/University of Gdansk English Language Centre. He is one of the authors of *Options for English* (Warsaw 1991). He is currently working full-time as a trainer at the College for Foreign Language Teachers at the University of Gdansk.

Hanna Kryszewska studied English at the University of Gdansk, where she gained the equivalent of an MA in Applied Linguistics. From 1979 to 1987 she taught English at the University of Gdansk English Language Centre, and since 1987 has been a Lecturer at the University. She has also taught on introductory English courses and teacher training courses at Pilgrims language school in Canterbury. She is one of the authors of *Options for English*, a book for teachers of English working with advanced students. She also works as a trainer at the College for Foreign Language Teachers.

Alan Maley worked for The British Council from 1962–1988, serving as English Language Officer in Yugoslavia, Ghana, Italy, France, and China, and as Regional Representative for The British Council in South India (Madras). He is currently Director-General of the Bell Educational Trust, Cambridge. He wrote *Quartet* (with Françoise Grellet and Wim Welsing, OUP 1982), and *Literature*, in this series (with Alan Duff, OUP 1990). He has also written *Beyond Words*, *Sounds Interesting*, *Sounds Intriguing*, *Words*, *Variations on a Theme*, and *Drama Techniques in Language Learning* (all with Alan Duff), *The Mind's Eye* (with Françoise Grellet and Alan Duff), and *Learning to Listen* and *Poem into Poem* (with Sandra Moulding). He is also Series Editor for the New Perspectives and Oxford Supplementary Skills series.

Foreword

In the kind of classrooms with which most of us are familiar it is normal and expected that teachers will make most, if not all, of the decisions about the teaching content and materials. And that, in a majority of cases, teaching will be based on some sort of published or pre-determined materials.

This book presents a radical alternative to both these assumptions.

In the first place, the learners take over much of the decision-making normally assigned to teachers. The approach makes learner-input central to the learning process. It is the learners themselves who become the major teaching resource. It shows how, by tapping into the knowledge and experience of the learners, the quality of the learning process is enhanced, since it becomes both more relevant and more deeply felt. There is a sense in which the teacher becomes a learner and learners are transformed into teachers.

In the second place there is a clear move away from dependence on the pre-determined content and format of published materials: every class will bring its own unique mix of individuals and their past experiences; every lesson will generate a unique set of needs. This freedom from dependence on sophisticated materials or technology makes the approach especially suitable for resource-poor environments, and it is perhaps no accident that the authors developed it in Poland where, at the time, access to such facilities was rare.

There are clear links between this approach and the current trend towards Learner Autonomy, Self-directed Learning, and Learner Independence. Perhaps unusually however, the emphasis here is on Learner Independence in the group mode rather than the individual self-study mode.

Among its ancillary advantages is its power as a tool for teacher development. No teacher taking this route can fail to develop both as a person and as a professional.

The approach offers an exciting and rewarding alternative to those teachers willing to try it. It undoubtedly takes courage to cast off from the security of control and pre-determined materials, to trust to the power of process and of learner-input, but the rewards are correspondingly great.

Alan Maley

Introduction

What is learner-based teaching?

The main principle in learner-based teaching is that all class activities can be done using information that the learners themselves bring to the class. All humanistic approaches to teaching accept that some language input can be based on the experience, knowledge, and expertise of individual students. What is novel about learner-based teaching is the idea that *all* activities can be based on that wealth of experience, be they grammar exercises, exam preparation, games, or translations.

The activities described in this book show teachers how to help their students to teach themselves, and each other, about English. Using a learner-based approach, the learners themselves are responsible for the information input, thereby ensuring its relevance and topicality for each particular group.

The basic procedure has two stages. In the first, learners prepare materials which are designed to practice, for example, a particular skill, function, or grammar item. In doing this, they draw on all the linguistic resources they already have. In the second stage, these materials are passed to other learners in the class who carry out the activities. In this way students obtain valuable language practice, not only while they are using the materials, but while they are preparing them as well.

How we arrived at learner-based teaching

We arrived at learner-based teaching along different routes but mainly in response to teaching conditions in Poland. Here, few teachers have access to a wide range of recently published materials. We found that people were dissatisfied with the repeated use of the same coursebooks. Many complained that the materials they had did not meet the real needs and interests of their students.

As a result, in the teacher-training sessions we ran we evolved the principle that the activities we developed should not require 'materials', equipment such as photocopiers, or a lot of preparation time. We eventually concluded that a lack of 'good materials' might, in fact, be a very positive and liberating thing.

A second factor was that some of the groups of students we taught consisted of academics of varying ages, with different specialities, who already possessed a good command of English. In certain areas their knowledge was often considerably greater than ours. This taught us to respect them as learners, and see them as individuals rather than as 'a class of foreign students', and to call upon their specialist knowledge in the lessons. For example, a physicist specializing in acoustics proved to be an invaluable source of information during a class on noise pollution. His expertise was available to be exploited and he was only too eager to co-operate.

Two other events set us thinking about learner-based teaching. One of these was a teacher-training session run for teachers of our Language Centre in Poland by John Morgan and Mario Rinvolucri. The second was using a manuscript of Chris Sion's *Inner Voice* (to be published in 1992 as *Talking to Yourself in English*) for group sessions. These stimuli made us realize how much potential resided in the students. Yet we had been complaining of the scarcity of topical and authentic material!

Most of the activities described in this book were developed while working with small groups (twelve to fourteen) of adult learners, others while working with small groups of children. Some of the activities may not work as well with larger groups and some may not work with students of particular ages. This is clearly indicated in the activities concerned. However, the *principles* of learner-based teaching can, we believe, be applied to groups of all sizes, ages, and levels.

As the learners themselves are the producers of the materials, they are likely to be suitable in terms of interest and level, whatever the group's size or composition.

What is the role of the teacher?

The teacher can be *an active participant* in the group, genuinely taking part in the activities, contributing ideas and opinions, or relating personal experiences.

The teacher is also *a helper and resource*, responding to learners' requests for help with vocabulary and grammar. By providing what the language students ask for, at the time they actually need it to express themselves, the teacher can facilitate more effective learning.

At other times the teacher is a *monitor*, checking what learners have produced before they pass it on to other learners. This is especially desirable in, for example, grammar and examination practice activities. In the book we suggest where such monitoring may be required. In some activities, however, like 'Invent a game' in Section 6, the teacher is advised not to correct what the learners have prepared. In this activity, students can see from what others do whether they have been successful in writing clearly and comprehensively. In other cases, the teacher can decide when to do the correcting. Instead of correcting during a lesson, it may be preferable to devote time later to a particular problem.

Whatever the activity, a learner-based approach is aimed at narrowing the traditional gap between teacher and student. In learner-based teaching, the teaching and the learning are taking place on both sides.

What about coursebooks?

The value of coursebooks as a vital learning tool is universally recognized. Our aim is not to reject the coursebook as a teaching aid, but rather to suggest ways of avoiding over-dependence on it. A pre-determined syllabus that underlies a coursebook can bypass the needs of students. Topic areas are pre-selected, which means that some will probably be of little or no interest to particular individuals. In some cases the information content is already over-familiar to students. In others it may be remote from their everyday reality.

A potential problem with following a coursebook is that students can, and do, read ahead to find out what is coming next. Learner-based teaching is unpredictable, and more likely to foster a heightened sense of curiosity.

The coursebook can co-exist comfortably with learner-based teaching. Our learners use it mainly at home for self-study, while in class time we concentrate on activating the language they have picked up from various sources, such as TV or newspapers, as well as their coursebook.

What are the advantages of using learner-based teaching?

1 The potential of the learner

Students bring a lot with them. They all have their own ideas, opinions, experiences, and areas of expertise. All of this is important to them. What they need from the English language classroom is the language to express all this, and thereby themselves, in English.

Learner-based teaching focuses on encouraging learners to express their ideas freely. This route to fluency is more direct than the teacher imposing irrelevant topics in the hope that with time learners will be able to say what they really want to.

All of the activities, even grammar practice, are based on the 'here and now' of the learners. If, for example, students wish to practice the present perfect, they do it using language which is relevant to them.

Apart from their individual interests and specialities, the learners bring their native language and culture to the classroom. Learner-based teaching encourages them to incorporate this into their target-language competence (see especially Section 5).

2   Constant needs analysis

The activities for a particular group are chosen to meet the current needs of its members. As students carry out an activity, teachers can spot the gaps in their target language competence and introduce suitable practice activities in subsequent lessons. In learner-based teaching, therefore, analysis is a continually developing process.

3   Topicality

Learner-based teaching allows us to introduce local or international issues and ideas which are of current interest to particular groups, for example, elections, cultural events, or scientific developments. Learner input may be especially important where there is no up-to-date English-language coverage of such topics available.

4   Previous learning experience

Students who have already been studying the language for some time in an environment where little published material is available complain of repetitiveness. A learner-based approach offers a much more open-ended experience. A framework is given, but the learners bear the responsibility for filling in the details, so that the same framework can evolve in completely different ways with different groups. Even a student who has worked with an activity before will make new discoveries when working in a different group.

5 Learners as authors

Language practice is doubled in learner-based teaching because learners are involved in preparing as well as using the practice materials. They are clearly interested in how others will use what they have prepared. For example, if groups of students prepare lists of words for other groups to use as the basis for writing a text, the 'authors' of the list will be interested in how their words have been exploited. They now have a real reason to pay attention in the reporting-back stage.

6 Pace

Teachers may feel disconcerted by the seemingly lengthy preparation work necessary. It may seem so much easier to hand out texts at the beginning of a lesson, rather than asking the learners to write their own. However, as the activity progresses, the pace increases. Also, the involvement of the learners is total throughout.

7 The element of surprise

As materials are not available in advance, there is a strong element of surprise. Not only do the learners not know what is coming before the lesson starts, but they are often unable to predict how the lesson will develop, and how the material they have produced will be used.

8 Peer teaching and correction

Students in a group often come from very different learning backgrounds. Even in groups with similar learning experiences there are always different levels of language competence. Learner-based teaching encourages students to work together and learn from each other. Activities are structured so that learners *have* to pay attention to what their colleagues are saying. They can teach and correct each other. Working together, the class can pool whatever individual linguistic resources they have, and work towards creating 'group grammars' and 'group lexicons'.

9 Group solidarity

The activities described in this book help to foster a spirit of group solidarity, in which everyone has a valid contribution to make, regardless of overall linguistic ability. Learners are working with one another, not in competition with one another.

What are the potential problems?

1 Learner resistance

Problems may arise with groups of learners who have specific preconceptions about the learning process. Some learners feel that they are learning only when talking or listening to the teacher, and do not see the benefit of working with other students. Some may have a competitive rather than a co-operative philosophy. Other learners may have a low opinion of themselves and feel that they cannot contribute to the lesson either in content or in knowledge of the target language. Some learners may simply not be interested in one another.

A gradual introduction, on an experimental basis, of learner-based activities may convince students of their value (see Section 8: 'How to think learner-based teaching'). It is possible, however, that there will be groups who will never accept an *exclusive* commitment to this approach. It is important for teachers to be sensitive to the opinions of their students before attempting to adopt a new way of working with them.

2 External restraints

Even if the teacher is required to follow an external syllabus, it may still be possible to cover parts of the syllabus using learner-based teaching activities. The same applies if students are preparing for an external examination (see Section 7: 'Exam preparation').

3 Demands on the teacher

Teachers using a learner-based approach are faced with the responsibility for the sequence of events in the classroom, a role which is normally left to the coursebook in conventional teaching. It is essential to keep a record of all work done: one way in which teachers and students can do this is by collaborating in the production of a regular class newsletter, which serves as a summary of all that has been achieved over a period of time, and reassures all concerned that progress is indeed being made.

In many of the activities the stages are interdependent. This means that the teacher must have a very clear idea of where the activity is leading, and how it is organized, and must give very accurate and precise instructions. If the learners are confused, they may not produce the material which is necessary for the activity to continue.

In spite of these demands, we hope that the benefits teachers find when they try some of these activities will persuade them to use more.

What is the role of learner-based teaching in the EFL syllabus?

Does it have to be 'all or nothing'? Not necessarily. Learner-based teaching can be any of the following:

– the one and only method used in the classroom. The activities practise skills, grammar, vocabulary, functions, and so on, and at the same time reveal needs to be met later with other activities.
– a complement to coursebooks, providing topicality, introducing special-interest topics and practising language not covered by the coursebook.
– an emergency kit to deal with unpredicted situations such as malfunctioning classroom hardware and poor attendance.

Realia, visual aids, and other classroom props

Learner-based teaching materials are by definition limited to those produced by the learners in class. Therefore paper and pen are usually all that is needed. The blackboard may be used as a group notepad, a focal point. Other pieces of classroom furniture can easily be exploited, as can walls and the floor, or any other available space.

On occasion, however, activities may benefit from the use of more sophisticated equipment such as photocopiers, audio or video recorders, or an OHP, but we would like to stress that these are always optional.

How to use this book

How the book is organized

The activities are divided into seven sections: 'Grammar', 'Vocabulary', 'Integrated skills', 'Writing', 'Translation', 'Games', 'Exam preparation'.

The section headings indicate where the main emphasis of the activities lies and where most time should be spent. If teachers want to concentrate on developing writing skills, for example, they should look at the activities under that section. If they want to practise a particular sub-skill, for example writing instructions, they should look through the Contents page under *Language focus*. However, it is very much in the nature of learner-based teaching that activities are mixed and varied. Games or vocabulary activities may contain an element of writing, grammar work may involve writing and game-playing. Writing instructions, for example, is an important part of the activities 'Invent a game' (6.10) and 'What shall we eat?' (2.8). Therefore, it is advisable to look under *Language focus* in all sections of the book when selecting activities. There is no linguistic progression within the sections of the book, so teachers are free to pick and choose as they wish.

How each activity is organized

Information for the teacher on each activity is presented under the following headings: *Title, Level, Time, Language focus*.

Some activities also have *Variations, Sample products*, and *Remarks*. The *Variations* suggest how activities can be expanded or contracted or how they may be given a different language focus. *Sample products* give examples of the materials which our students in Poland actually prepared in the course of a lesson. We have provided these wherever we felt they would clarify how a particular activity works. The materials are presented in the form in which they were used in the lesson. This means that sometimes they were corrected and sometimes not, depending on the type of activity. The *Remarks* are mainly concerned with pointing out potential difficulties in conducting the activity.

Teachers may choose to use an activity in its entirety, or only part of it, depending on the needs of the students, their interests, and on the time available. If the activity is used in its entirety, this may be within one lesson, or spread over two or more lessons. In the latter case, teachers can use the time between lessons to check the material produced by the learners.

To teachers of other languages

The activities in this book were developed with students learning English as a foreign language. However, most of them, with the possible exception of some of the grammar activities, could be used without any adaptation with students learning other languages.

To teachers of English as a first language

All of the activities can be used with native speaker students of English at school level or beyond, to help develop their language skills and their confidence in using the language.

A final word

We hope that teachers and learners using the activities described in this book will find them stimulating and effective.

Teachers may find that they have to adapt some of the activities in this book to suit their classes and teaching conditions. Our main hope, however, is that having explored the activities and reflected on the questions in Section 8, 'How to think learner-based teaching', teachers will become independent of this book too, and begin to devise their own activities to use with particular groups, based on the principles of learner-based teaching.

1 Grammar exercises and drills

Introduction

The grammar practice activities take various forms and perform different functions. The activities are structured around three different aspects of grammar work:

1 Tasks requiring learners to use a particular structure or language point

These activities are structured in such a way that, in order to carry out the task set by the teacher, learners are obliged to use a particular structure or structures. The language points chosen by the teacher are either new or relatively new structures which need reinforcing, or ones that have caused problems in the past and require more attention.

2 Tasks structured to exploit a more general notion, such as past time

This is an implicit approach and activities are structured in such a way that learners revise a wider area of the language than in point 1. There is no explicit focus on grammar and the learners may not even realize what they are practising. In order to carry out the task learners have to use whatever language they know. Through these tasks the teacher activates the knowledge the learners have, but often do not use, or reveals gaps in their knowledge and areas for further work.

3 Tasks drawing upon the learners' formal knowledge of the target language and its grammar rules

This area of grammar work focuses the learners' attention on their understanding of grammatical rules in the target language. In these tasks learners pool their knowledge of the rules and arrive at an explicit 'Group grammar book'. The activities encourage peer teaching and correction. In this way group work can genuinely become cooperative language learning.

At the same time the activities help learners to establish a common language necessary to talk about the language. By learning the metalanguage, they take the first step towards understanding and making more effective use of formal grammar books, reference books, and dictionaries.

1.1   Decisions

LEVEL

Upper intermediate

TIME

30–40 minutes

LANGUAGE

Mixed conditionals

PROCEDURE

1 Tell the class about a significant decision that you have made in your life.
For example: 'I was sitting in a pub in Brighton one night thinking about where my career was going. At that time I was teaching in Italy. I was keen to do a second degree but I didn't think I could afford it and I was sure I wouldn't get a grant to do it. I met a friend of a friend in the pub who told me that he had just finished his MA degree, that he had the same first degree as I had and he had received a grant. He encouraged me to apply for one. I did. I got it. I completed the degree, and as a result of that I'm living and working in Poland'.

2 In their exercise books learners then briefly describe a significant decision *they* have made in their lives.

3 When they have all finished, they first comment on your decision including the word *if* in their remarks.

4 Write some of the comments on the board to illustrate the variety of conditional forms possible. For example, learners in one class came up with such examples as:

If you hadn't met that man, you wouldn't have applied for a grant.
If you hadn't done the MA, you wouldn't be living in Poland.
If you hadn't gone to the pub, you might not be living here now.

5 Learners now circulate, reading out their own decision and inviting different partners in turn to comment on it, using *if*. They in turn comment in the same way on their partners' decisions.

6 When they have finished milling around, encourage them to sit down and quietly repeat to themselves the various comments they have made and heard.

VARIATION

In larger groups, or where the arrangement of the classroom does not permit milling around, learners can write their decisions on pieces of paper and circulate them, so that other people in the room can write comments. You might stipulate that learners are not to repeat comments already made on a decision, so they have to read what others have written. This gives them exposure to more examples of conditional forms and at the same time requires them to dig more deeply into their imaginative resources.

REMARKS

1 The decision that you tell the class about does not have to be a significant turning point in your life. If it is, it might actually discourage learners from commenting. It could be of a more everyday nature, for example, *I bought a new coat yesterday, I went to a new disco last night, I came home really late last night.* Your model should also take into account the age and experience of the learners.

2 Point out that when the learners write down their own decision it should be one they have already acted on and not one still requiring action.

3 In stage 5 learners will be correcting each other. To begin with they may call on you for help but as this stage develops they become more confident about correcting others.

4 As this is an interactive exercise all the learners will be attending to what is going on all the time, otherwise the activity cannot happen. This is rarely the case when grammar exercises are done orally around the class and where learners may switch off once they have had their turn.

1.2 From 'a' to 'the'

LEVEL

Lower-intermediate and above

TIME

45–60 minutes

LANGUAGE

Use of definite and indefinite articles

PROCEDURE

1 Learners work in pairs and write down all the rules concerning the use of articles they can remember.

2 They put the lists aside and write a text on a given everyday subject, for example 'Mr Smith's last holiday', in which they apply all the rules they have remembered. Make sure that the texts are correct both in terms of general language and in the use of articles.

3 All the texts are displayed on the wall. Still in the same pairs, learners walk around and read other texts, ticking off on their lists those rules that are exemplified.

4 Prepare a list of rules you think the learners will know or recognize. While they are working on stages 2 and 3, look at their texts and tick the rules on your list that have been applied.

5 Plan your own story which will continue on from one of the texts and incorporate rules *not* already used by the learners.

6 The learners sit down. They listen to the continuing story of 'Mr Smith' and identify more rules.

7 Elicit from the class the rules they think they have identified.

SAMPLE PRODUCT   Learners

Mr. Smith decided to go on holiday to the seaside . It was a change because he usually goes along the Vistula river to the Tatra mountains, taking the whole family with him. On arrival the first thing he did was to look for a restaurant. He chose the nearest. He had a quarrel with a friend of his there. They were both taken to prison and charged with grievous bodily harm, but were soon released on bail . During their stay in prison, their wives came to the prison to pay them a short visit . They informed their husbands that this way of spending a holiday separately was quite nice — and worth repeating .

Teacher

After some time Mr. Smith wanted to go home. He boarded the plane and to his surprise, he found himself sitting near a beautiful woman. They started talking and after some time the woman introduced herself. 'My name is Wilde', she said proudly. 'Well, my name is Smith', Mr. Smith replied. 'Not very rare names', he observed.

The flight passed pleasantly with banal exchanges about the weather and airline food. Mr. Smith was very helpful when his pretty neighbour felt unwell and he asked for a glass of juice from the flight attendant. Well, to be exact, it was a plastic cup. Under the new regulations glass is no longer allowed on planes. After touchdown he lost sight of Mrs. Wilde. He wasn't worried in the least. He travelled home on a very crowded Underground.

Some days later he was telling a friend of his about the encounter. 'I met a Mrs. Wilde on the plane, a very beautiful woman, blonde, long legs...' Mr. Smith began to reminisce. 'My God! A Mrs. Wilde! What a joke!' the friend exclaimed. 'It was the Mrs. Wilde! Kim Wilde! She was travelling on the same plane as you were!' 'That's possible. The face seemed familiar...' Mr. Smith replied unnerved. 'So what?'

VARIATION 1

In more advanced groups or in groups that generally find it difficult to talk about grammar, learners may write the texts without first writing down the rules. Stage 1 is then omitted and in stage 3 they only read the texts. In this case learners use their general knowledge of grammar and the exercise is more of an awareness exercise.

VARIATION 2

If you are more adventurous, you may like to improvise the continuation of the story without preparing a list as in stage 4.

VARIATION 3

If learners cannot remember many rules in stage 1, they can compare and collate their lists *before* the activity proceeds to stage 2.

VARIATION 4

In stage 3, instead of ticking off rules, learners can add new rules from other texts to their own lists, thereby building up their own grammar book.

REMARKS

1 This activity teaches learners to talk about grammar and helps them to learn to formulate grammar rules and consequently to understand them better when they encounter them in grammar books.

2 At the listening stage, by continuing the story you implicitly remind the learners of rules or introduce new ones. They often react with a physical movement when recognizing a familiar rule. They can also try to formulate new rules, usually by talking to the person they worked with before.

1.3 I know what my teacher has done

LEVEL

Lower-intermediate

TIME

20–40 minutes

LANGUAGE

Present perfect

PROCEDURE

1 The learners, working individually, write down ten questions addressed to you using the present perfect. The questions should be ones to which they expect the answer 'yes'. For example, *Have you been to London? Have you ever eaten a hamburger? Have you brushed your teeth today?*

2 Learners fire the questions at you as quickly as possible.

3 They keep a record of their score, one point for each 'yes' answer they get from you. They are not allowed to repeat a question someone else has already asked, and they only score points for the questions they themselves have asked. If someone else asks a question they have written down, they get no score.

4 The student with the most points is the winner. The other learners can speculate about why that person knows you so well . . .

5 Then learners form pairs. Individually they write down ten more present perfect questions addressed to their partner to which they expect the answer 'no'.

6 In pairs they ask and answer the questions, scoring one point for every 'no' answer they receive.

VARIATION   Instead of stage 4, you can ask the learners to recall what you have *not* actually done.

REMARKS   This activity may work better if the class already knows you quite well.

1.4 Random comparisons

LEVEL   **Lower-intermediate and above**

TIME   **15–30 minutes**

LANGUAGE   **Comparative adjectives**

PROCEDURE   **1** Learners write down ten nouns on a separate piece of paper. These can be either abstract or concrete nouns.

2 Collect these pieces of paper.

3 On another piece of paper learners write a second set of 10 nouns.

4 Collect these pieces of paper.

5 Pair off the learners.

6 Shuffle the papers and give out two to each pair.

7 Learners write ten comparative sentences using the first noun from the first list and the first noun from the second and so on. For example, in one class the nouns *Way* and *Heaven* produced this sentence: *The way to Heaven is more difficult than the road to Hell.* Other examples were: *It's easier to write on a typewriter than with a pen* (from *pen* and *typewriter*); *True love is as strong and enduring as an oak tree* (from *love* and *tree*).

8 The pairs read out their sentences to the class for their comments.

REMARKS   The random factor in choosing items for comparison can lead to more imaginative and interesting practice, but it may require a sense of the absurd.

1.5 Character building

LEVEL   Elementary

TIME   20–30 minutes

LANGUAGE   Simple present

PROCEDURE
1 Draw a circle on the board.

2 Tell the learners they are going to build this into a character.

3 Ask them first of all whether it's a man or a woman.

4 Continue to ask questions to build up the physical representation on the board. For example, *Does he have a moustache? Is he fat? Does she have a big nose?*

5 Continue to ask questions (but without adding to the drawing) about where the person lives, their job, interests, family, and so on, and point out any apparent contradictions, for example, *Well, if he's so interested in sport, how come he's fat? She's only 28 and she's got ten children?*

VARIATION   Reverse the roles. Now learners ask you questions enabling you to build up a character. Ask a student to do the drawing on the blackboard so you have an opportunity to introduce or revise comparisons, for example, *No, he's not that tall*, or *Her hair's longer than that.*

REMARKS   The drawing on the board helps to suggest a character and serves as the basis for the subsequent work. As learners come up with suggestions, the pace increases and the learners themselves point out contradictions and suggest alternatives.

1.6 My country/district

LEVEL   Elementary

TIME   20 minutes

LANGUAGE   'Can' (possibility)

PROCEDURE
1 Learners get into groups according to where they live. Two or three is probably best.

2 Explain to the learners that there will be a competition to choose which is the best country or district to live in from the point of view of the facilities it offers.

3 In their groups learners then prepare a list of things they can do in their country or district, for example, *You can go skiing in Switzerland, You can walk by the sea in Gdynia, You can go to a Chinese restaurant in Hong Kong.*

4 In turn groups read out their lists. The other groups can challenge or ask for more information, for example, *Where can you walk by the sea in Gdynia?*

5 The activity can be a game with groups scoring one point for each facility or amenity, provided that this is not contested by the opposing group. The group with the most points wins.

VARIATION	With multilingual groups the class could be divided according to countries, but one would have to be careful that this did not lead to the expression of strong antagonistic feelings. On courses where students are away from home, they could be divided according to where their lodgings are.
REMARKS	1 There is a certain amount of local rivalry but the 'competition' is very good-natured and the exercise surprisingly productive. 2 The language used can be very varied, especially as discussion gets more heated. The activity does not have to be restricted to practising 'can'.

1.7 Controversial questions

LEVEL	Intermediate and above
TIME	20–40 minutes
LANGUAGE	Passive in simple past
PROCEDURE	1 Divide the class into groups of about four or five people. 2 The learners are to prepare four controversial questions using the passive voice in the simple past, for example *Was John F. Kennedy assassinated by Lee Oswald?* 3 The groups take it in turns to ask their questions, which the other groups discuss and answer. You act as the official time-keeper, noting how long learners spend discussing each question. 4 The winning group is the one whose questions provoke the longest total discussion time.
SAMPLE PRODUCT	On a course run for workers at Solidarity headquarters in Gdansk, Poland, the students spent a lot of time discussing such questions as: 1 Why was Walesa imprisoned? A lot of the discussion centred on whether *interned* is the same as *imprisoned.*

2 When was Walesa elected leader of Solidarity?
There was considerable discussion about whether *proclaimed* means the same as *elected* and about whether *chairman* is the same as *leader*.

1.8 The wonderful world of inventions

LEVEL

Lower-intermediate and above

TIME

30–45 minutes

LANGUAGE

Talking about past events

PROCEDURE

1 Learners individually write down the three inventions they consider most important in the history of humanity.

2 Fix a long piece of paper/wallpaper to the wall and draw a horizontal line, marking '0. Anno Domini' in the middle. Alternatively, this could be drawn on the board.

3 All the learners together write their inventions in the correct chronological place above the line, paying due attention to what has already been written. If space is limited, learners can write the inventions vertically, for example:

4 Learners go back to their places, and either in small groups or as a whole class agree on the sequencing of the inventions, and suggest possible amendments.

5 Once the final version has been decided on, select a few inventions at random and encourage discussion of what life was like before they were invented. This focuses the learners' attention on the task to follow.

6 Divide the class into small groups of three or four, and give a cut-up section of the paper to each group. Learners write a paragraph describing life then and the changes which the inventions introduced.

7 When the descriptions are ready, the fragments are reassembled on the wall. Give the class an opportunity to read the texts. Usually a discussion follows.

SAMPLE PRODUCT

People were not
able to fight germs
and bacteria and
minor infections
often caused death.

Many people
died because of
Tuberculosis and
other infectious diseases.
high death rate.

Before radar was invented
there were a lot of
collisions at sea.
With radar ships
could manoeuvre
more safely in bad
weather conditions.
It was used to locate
enemy vessels and it
was easier to flee the
enemy.

PENICILLIN

RADAR

It enabled fishermen
to locate shoals of fish
which otherwise would
remain unnoticed and
alive.

VARIATION 1

If the class is small, up to about fifteen, and if a drill is required, learners write the inventions on the blackboard, and then stand under one of them. They make statements on what life used to be like or what people did before the particular inventions.

VARIATION 2

The activity can be expanded by asking the learners to think of 'future' inventions and write them on a line extended into the future. In the writing stage this leads to the use of future perfect and future progressive forms. This variation means that learners are not only exploiting their knowledge of the world but also using their imagination, and using future tenses.

VARIATION 3

Conditionals can be practised by asking learners to describe what life would be like if certain things had not been invented.

VARIATION 4

If no suitable paper is available, learners can write the inventions on the board. Later assign them particular sections of the line to work on. They write their texts on pieces of paper, which are assembled in the appropriate order as a wall display. Alternatively students could arrange the pieces of paper on the floor. Prepare one slip with '0. Anno Domini' written on it. Place it on the floor and draw an imaginary line, or use a floorboard, or line of the carpet as the time line.

REMARKS

In stage 4 it is not necessary that the sequence is historically correct in every detail. It is important that the group agrees on a sequence. As a follow-up, students can check the sequence out of class.

Before nuclear power
energy was obtained
from coal or fuels
and it was safer.
Pollution (in case of
emergency) is smaller
than in case of
nuclear energy which
causes entire disaster
of biological environment.

Less noise, music
was calmer, more
romantic.

Movement on the stage:
audience was more
involved and engaged
in the show.

It made possible
various transmissions
and flow of
information of
all kinds.

NUCLEAR POWER   ELECTRIC GUITAR   TELECOMMUNICATIONS

TODAY

War threat,
total
annihilation
of life
on earth.

New stage
of the development
of Pop music
and the birth
of Rock.

1.9 Is that right?

LEVEL

Elementary and above

TIME

15–20 mintues

LANGUAGE

Confirming

PROCEDURE

1 Each learner takes a piece of paper and folds it vertically in two.

2 On one side learners write the heading *I like*, and on the other *I don't like*.

3 Under each heading they write five things or activities they really like and dislike.

4 Learners then get into pairs and exchange their pieces of paper.

5 Student A first makes some statements in any order about the other student, using the information from both columns, and student B has to confirm it.

The exchanges take the following form:
A: *You like milk.*
B: *Yes, I do.*
A: *You don't like tea.*
B: *No, I don't.*
A: *You don't like your mother's cat.*
B: *No, I don't.*

6 They reverse roles.

VARIATION 1	The subject and the grammar point of this drill can change depending on the topics you choose, for example, things the learner can/cannot do, places visited/not visited, things they will/won't do at the weekend.

VARIATION 2	With more advanced learners the task can be made more complicated. When choosing from the list, student A may alter the information from student's B list, for example, student B likes milk, and student A says *You don't like milk*. Then a new response is introduced and student B has to respond *But I do/I do like milk*.

REMARKS

1 For this activity to be a meaningful drill it is crucial for learners to write true facts about themselves, otherwise they would be unable to respond quickly and correctly without consulting their own sheet.

2 In some languages to confirm that a negative statement is true you say *yes*, for example: *You don't like whisky.*
★Yes, I don't.
This drill is useful for learners whose native language works in this way.

3 This drill is also useful for practising stress patterns.

1.10 My grammar problem

LEVEL　　　　**Lower-intermediate and above**

TIME　　　　**45–60 minutes**

LANGUAGE　　　　**Learners' problems**

PROCEDURE

1 Ask each student to identify a grammar problem they have or think they have. To make the task easier tell the learners they may browse through their exercise books and recent homework.

2 Check that every student has got at least one problem.

3 Ask learners to mill around to see if they can find anyone with a similar problem or problems. The idea is that they should form pairs with related grammar problems. For example, various conditionals and mixed conditionals could pair up, or reported statements and questions, or passive and 'have something done' constructions.

4 Ask each pair to write down their problem on a piece of paper, for example 'conditionals'. They should write the grammatical term and also one example sentence. The problems are then displayed.

5 Each pair then chooses from this selection a problem they think they understand—a different problem for each pair.

6 Using reference books, grammar books, and the teacher, they prepare an explanation or mini-lecture on the problem. The teacher can answer specific questions but should not offer a complete explanation of the problem.

7 Each pair presents their lecture to the whole class. Others may challenge or ask for clarification. If the students cannot agree, or if the explanations are inaccurate or incomplete, add to or amend what they have said.

VARIATION 1

If it is a large class, instead of forming pairs at stage 3, form groups of three or four, so that there will be fewer presentations in the last stage.

VARIATION 2

For stage 7 split the pairs and ask the learners to form two big circles. Working clockwise, learners present their lecture to their neighbour, who passes it on. The activity ends when the explanations come full circle and the originator sees if the lecture has been simplified too much or misunderstood. If so, they may have to explain their reservations to their circle.

VARIATION 3

After stage 3 ask each pair or group to write a sentence containing the problem. They write the sentence in the middle of a sheet of paper. Redistribute the sheets. Another pair then has to write a short story, the central part of which is the problem sentence. Remove the problem sentence by cutting it out or erasing it. The stories circulate and each pair has to try to reconstruct the missing sentence. The stories, the original problem sentence, and the suggested sentences are displayed. Discuss the outcome with the class.

VARIATION 4

If students cannot find partners in stage 3, they should form pairs with any other student and try to incorporate both the problems in one sentence.

SAMPLE PRODUCT

(from Variation 3)

Problem sentence:
The agreement having been signed, the ministers left the room.

The story:

The Ministry Hall was crowded, full of journalists and observers waiting for the result of the meeting. The agreement having been signed, the ministers left the room. It was a great success for both of them as they hadn't expected such a solution. It was the start of good co-operation between two antagonistic countries.

REMARKS

1 The activity and the variation show ways in which the learners can provide formal and practical grammar explanations to help others in the class with their problems.

2 It is possible that students will come up with the same problems, in which case more than one pair may be working on a presentation of, say, the present perfect. This is not a problem. It will make for even more informed discussion in the last stage.

3 You may have to help students with terminology when they are naming their problems.

2 Vocabulary

Introduction

The activities in this section aim at expanding vocabulary through:

– learning new words from other learners
– activating the individual's passive vocabulary
– browsing through dictionaries with a specific purpose, provided by the frame of the activity
– looking up specific words in bilingual dictionaries
– learning from the teacher (but only those words that learners specifically ask for).

The activities are structured in such a way that they reveal lexical gaps and give learners a chance to fill them. The students therefore have more control over what they learn. The topic area used is one that is introduced by the teacher, but within that area it is the students who decide which words they want to learn and not the teacher or the syllabus. They choose words which are important for them and which are part of their first language lexicon. In this way the activities help to approximate the target language lexicon of the learners to that of their first language.

In filling lexical gaps, students can learn from each other, or from the teacher, or make use of monolingual or bilingual dictionaries. Monolingual dictionaries can be used for 'purposeful browsing' (see 'Beat the expert' (2.2,) Variation 1) and bilingual dictionaries for finding specific words. Even if teachers and learners have the same first language, the bilingual dictionary may be important. Learners may have particular areas of experience or knowledge which mean that they know words in the native language that the teacher does not.

2.1 Dr Jekyll and Mr Hyde

LEVEL	**Intermediate and above**
TIME	**60–70 minutes**
LANGUAGE	**Adjectives of character and physique**
PROCEDURE	1 Learners form small groups of two or three people so that there is an even number of groups.

2 Each group prepares a written A–Z of adjectives of character and physique, that is they write down the letters of the alphabet and write one adjective beginning with each letter, for example *aggressive, brave, clever*, and so on.

3 Collect the lists and re-distribute them to different groups.

4 The groups now prepare to 'build' a person. To do this, they go through their new list and cross out contradictory adjectives. For example, if a list has the words *anxious* and *confident*, the learners have to decide which one of them to delete.

5 Once the learners have produced 'internally consistent' lists, they pass on their lists to another group.

6 Write on the board, or dictate, the following headings:

sex	spent last holiday in
age	lives in
education	hobby
profession	pet hate
nationality	greatest dream
family status	

Using the list of adjectives they have received, the groups try to imagine the person described and complete a 'curriculum vitae' for that person.

7 Pair off the groups. Each group takes it in turn to describe their character to the second group, who may ask for clarification or elaboration. As they listen, learners take notes.

8 Remind the learners of, or elicit from them, the story of Dr Jekyll and Mr Hyde, emphasizing the idea of the sudden and complete transformation of character after a particular event: *Previously he was respectable, but when he took the potion he became a devil.*

9 The groups now work with the new characters, that is the one they have heard described. They think of how this character could change having taken the potion. They prepare an oral presentation, or as a group write a paragraph including the sentence: *But when he/she took the potion . . .*

10 Back in their paired groups from stage 7, learners read the paragraphs back to the creators of the original character.

SAMPLE PRODUCT   Stage 1

active	frank	keen	opportunistic	shy	willing
bold	generous	loyal	proud	tall	x...
cunning	hysterical	mean	quarrelsome	ugly	youthful
diabolical	ingenious	nervous	righteous	violent	zealous
eccentric	jealous				

Stage 6

Name:	Deco Antonov	SEX	male
AGE	25	EDUCATION	primary school
PROFESSION	personal assistant	NATIONALITY	Bulgarian of Turkish origin
FAMILY STATUS	single	HOBBY	football, circus
PET HATE	books, very educated people	LAST HOLIDAY	in prison in Paris
LIVES	with his mother in Turkey	GREATEST DREAM	to become President

Stage 9 (Variation 2)

Once in the depths of Bulgaria there was a man. He was a huge, strong man with a long scar on his forehead. He was about 25 and worked as a personal assistant. He was still single. No woman in the neighbourhood wanted such a cruel guy as a husband. He didn't like books or too educated people. Once he decided to kill his former teacher.

He was caught on the spot and imprisoned. It had always been his ambition to become president and there, in prison, he realized that he must change to achieve this. He started reading books on politics and good manners. When he read *The Prince* by Machiavelli, he suddenly changed. He started to organize life in prison. He established a culture club and a historical discussion club. He kept saying that violence was not the way. He became the best adviser of the chief of the prison and the favourite friend of all the prisoners. He was released.

VARIATION 1　　　If your class have problems distinguishing between: *What does he look like?* and *What's he like?* you can introduce a drill in stage 2. When they have written out their lists, learners can go through them writing or saying the appropriate question for each adjective, for example: intelligent—*What's he like?*
　　　　　　　　　　　　　　　　　handsome—*What does he look like?*

VARIATION 2　　　In stage 9 learners can introduce an alternative to the potion to explain the transformation in character.

VARIATION 3　　　To expand the vocabulary work in stage 1, you can tell learners to write a list of three adjectives for each letter. Later they cross out the first two and continue working with the remaining one. In this way learners will be working with those adjectives they had to search for, either in their memories or in a monolingual dictionary, and not the first words that came to mind.

REMARKS　　　1 The starting point for this exercise is a string of words triggered by the alphabet. Only later does the activity develop into a communicative one. This apparently restrictive technique is a very good way of organizing and eliciting random language which will provide the basis for further work, such as creative writing, vocabulary development, or grammar (see 1.4 and 4.1).

2 In stage 9 the focus can be either on strict antonyms or freer opposites, depending on the instructions you give.

3 This is a relatively long activity and you may decide not to follow it through to the end. It is possible to stop the activity either after stage 5 or stage 7.

2.2 Beat the expert

LEVEL

Intermediate and above

TIME

30–45 minutes

LANGUAGE

Expansion of topic vocabulary

PROCEDURE

1 Each learner thinks of a non-professional topic or skill they know a lot about, for example, 'making clothes', 'wildlife', 'air travel in Africa', 'battleships of World War II'.

2 They then take a sheet of paper and fold it like this:

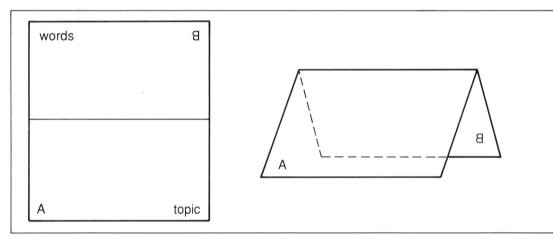

They write the topic of their expertise on side A, and a list of ten words that are related to the topic on side B.

3 When the lists are ready the learners mill around displaying side A of their sheets. They form pairs at random and one learner reads the topic their partner has written on side A and then the list of words on side B.

4 Next, still in pairs, the learners try to challenge each other by asking the 'experts' for words which they think they should know in English. They can do this by giving the word in their native language (in monolingual groups), or by giving an explanation, for example *'What do you call the thing that covers the car engine?'*. If the 'experts' know the words in English, they add them to their list in English, and if not, they add them in the native language. In this way they keep a record of the challenges.

5 Still in the same pairs, the learners reverse roles.

6 The challenges continue until everyone has challenged a given number of people.

7 Display the B sides, that is, those with the lists of words, on a wall or a blackboard. Learners read the words and try to:
a. recall what topic area the words come from
b. fill in words they know in English which are given in the native language of the learners.

8 As a follow-up, as homework or as a group activity, learners find English equivalents for the words they still do not know.

SAMPLE PRODUCT

Stage 1 Topic:
housebuilding

Stage 2 Words:
basement, bricks, cement, carpentry, plaster, sand, heat insulation, roof tiles, concrete mixer, window frames

Stage 4 Words added:
scaffolding, beam, threshold, pillars

VARIATION 1

You can vary stage 2. Either the learners list words they already know, or they can consult you or a bilingual dictionary. You can set a limit on the number of words to be looked up, for example three. Learners should avoid pictorial dictionaries where it is impossible to look up one lexical item at a time because the learner is confronted with a whole lexical field and can be swamped by too many new words. The emphasis in this activity is on the learners activating passively known vocabulary or selecting words which are important to them.

VARIATION 2

Learners can prepare a second topic of expertise at home and then challenge each other in class. They score points for each word they know in English that the 'expert' does not.

VARIATION 3

If the choice of topics for expertise is limited because the learners share the same interests, or have the same profession, the activity can be used for various types of revision. For example, give each learner a thematic area that has already been covered in class, such as 'shopping', 'disasters', or 'travelling'. In this way you can recycle previous language input.

REMARKS

1 In stage 2 learners should be trying to list words which others are unlikely to know, rather than obvious ones. For example, if the topic is 'Bringing up babies' the words should not be: *baby, little, mother*, but: *nanny, pram, nappy*.

2 We have described this activity as carried out with monolingual groups. In the case of multilingual groups, the challenging of the experts could be done completely in English, with learners referring to bilingual dictionaries. If, however, there is a pair sharing the same native language, they could use it in the challenging stage (stage 4).

2.3 Telephone numbers

LEVEL

All levels

TIME

15–20 minutes

LANGUAGE

Numbers and telephone language

PROCEDURE

1 Learners write down on a separate piece of paper all the telephone numbers they carry around in their heads—or imaginary ones if this is too embarrassing.

2 They form pairs and exchange papers with their partner.

3 They sit back to back and, selecting numbers from the other person's list, make up dialogues.

A possible conversation:

Student A (makes a ringing tone)
Student B (answers) *Hello*
Student A (checks the number) *Hello, is that 312799?*
Student B (confirms) *Yes*
Student A (asks for B by name) *Can I speak to Robert please?*
Student B (continues according to the telephone number given)
Robert doesn't live here, I'm his aunt, or
Mr. Wilson isn't here at the moment, but I'm his secretary. Can I take a message?

2.4 Make your own picture dictionary

LEVEL

Lower-intermediate and above

TIME

20 minutes

LANGUAGE

Identifying lexical gaps in easy-to-draw lexical fields

PROCEDURE

1 Give students a topic which is easy to draw, for example 'car' or 'tree'. In their exercise books, or on a piece of paper, they draw the object, but they can only include in the drawing the parts they know the names of in English. This activity works for all easily drawn lexical fields, for example, parts of the body (exterior or interior), machines, landscapes, and so on.

2 Learners circulate, looking at other people's drawings and asking the names of parts which they themselves do not know.

3 As they learn the new words they can add to their drawing until it is as complete as they want. Some learners will want a more detailed drawing than others.

4 Learners now label the parts whose names they did not know before.

VARIATION 1

Students think of their favourite animal and on a slip of paper write the name of a part of its body which somehow distinguishes it, for example 'wings'. They may have to refer to dictionaries for this. Collect the slips and form the class into large groups of eight to ten. Redistribute the slips so that each person gets one. Students look at all the words they have in their group and, either as a whole group or in sub-groups, draw and label the composite animal. Do not worry if the same word appears more than once. The resulting animal will simply be more exotic. Students give it a name and write a short paragraph describing the lifestyle of the animal and, if it is extinct, explaining why it became extinct.

SAMPLE PRODUCT

frog's eyes

bat's wings

fish's legs

FROGOBAT

A very strange creature was discovered by our reporter, Johnny Cymbalski, in his coffee. It has bat's wings and frog's eyes. It also has something like fish's legs. It is quite friendly, but if you don't give it a ticket to the cinema, it might bite you. It only drinks coffee and only eats pens. Oh, here is Johnny with the creature now. He calls it the Frogobat because of its eyes and wings. Sorry, I can't write any more because it ate my pen and Sara doesn't want to lend me hers. This is Andrew Ciolek, your CNN reporter.

VARIATION 2

Students themselves can decide what topic they want to draw. It could be a sport they like doing, a favourite place, such as the beach, or something connected with a hobby. They continue as above. If students are interested in other people's topics, give them time to copy and label each others' drawings. In this way learners can build up their own picture dictionary.

VARIATION 3

Ask the students to write a given number of words connected with an easily drawn topic, such as the human body, each on a separate piece of paper. Collect these and redistribute them. The whole class place their pieces of paper on the floor (or stick them on a wall) to reconstruct the body. They can discuss the accuracy of the placements. They can also place blank pieces of paper at points where parts are 'missing' and invite other students to name the parts. If no-one knows they can refer to a dictionary.

2.5 Finish my family tree

LEVEL

Elementary and lower-intermediate

TIME

20 minutes

LANGUAGE

Families and 'have got'

PROCEDURE

1 Check that the class know what a family tree looks like.

2 Ask the learners to write their own name in the middle of a clean sheet of paper.

3 Tell them they have 60 seconds to draw as much of their family tree as possible.

4 When the time is up pair them off and get them to exchange their incomplete trees.

5 In turns they ask the other person questions about their family and use the answers to complete the partner's family tree. For example, *Did your grandfather have any brothers? Was your uncle married? What are your nephews called?*

6 As they do the exercise they will ask you to fill in gaps in their vocabulary, for example *My father's brother is my . . .? — Uncle.*

VARIATION

The completed trees can form the basis of other activities. For example, in pairs students look at their partner's family trees and test how well they know their relatives by asking questions such as *Do you remember the date of your uncle's birthday? Can your cousin ski? What is your aunt's favourite drink?* One student continues to ask questions until the other is not able to give an answer. Then the roles are reversed.

2.6 Random phrasal verbs

LEVEL Intermediate

TIME 45 minutes

LANGUAGE Phrasal verbs

PROCEDURE 1 Each learner has to think of two prepositions that often combine with verbs to form phrasal verbs, for example *on* (*come on*); *off* (*go off*).

2 They write the prepositions on the board. Erase repetitions.

3 Give them a verb that combines with some (but not all) of these prepositions to form phrasal verbs.

4 Working in pairs or groups of three, they then discuss which prepositions this verb combines with to form phrasal verbs, and what they mean.

5 The groups report back on their discussions.

6 Give out dictionaries so that learners can check if they are right and also find other meanings for the phrasal verbs they thought of. Students should check only the phrasal verbs they thought of in their group; they should not start browsing through the other phrasal verbs in the dictionary.

7 Take away the dictionaries and ask the learners to put away their notes. In pairs learners write a short story, using a certain number, for example four, of the phrasal verbs they thought of in stage 4 or learned in stage 6.

8 While they are writing check that the use of both phrasal verbs and the language in general are correct.

9 Each pair in turn reads out their story, but leaving a pause or making a noise instead of reading out the phrasal verb.

10 As they listen to the stories, the other students individually write down the phrasal verbs they think are missing.

11 The authors of the stories read out the full versions so that the others can check their answers.

SAMPLE PRODUCT Prepositions suggested by the group:
by, at, out, for, over, on, up, off, in, around, away, through.

Verb given by the teacher: *get*, which combines to form phrasal verbs with all of the above except *for*, *in*, and *through*.

The text written by the students used *get at, get on, get around, get over*, and one not previously mentioned: *get away with* (see overleaf).

A politician was returning home from a party where he had spent a pleasant evening but had had quite a lot to drink. His wife suggested that he shouldn't drive but he was confident that nothing would happen, and that even if they were stopped by the police, he could _get away with_ it. As they were passing the hospital they were ~~stoped~~ stopped by the police. The politician tried to _get around_ the policeman by telling him who he was, but to no avail. He suggested to the policeman that he was unlikely to _get on_ in his career if he made trouble for important people. The policeman did not like being _got at_ in this way and took the politician to the police station. The politician was later convicted of drunken ~~driving~~ driving and lost his licence for two years. It took him even longer to _get over_ the blow to his pride.

VARIATION 1

Instead of a story learners can write a dialogue or a poem. Learning the poems by heart can help students to come to terms with phrasal verbs. In this case every student should be given a copy of the poems or they should be exhibited for a while so that learners can copy them. The problem with dialogue-writing may be that the dialogues, especially if they are short, can sound contrived.

VARIATION 2

Learners look at the prepositions on the blackboard and try to build phrasal verbs containing two prepositions, for example, _get away with_.

VARIATION 3

Learners prepare two sets of cards in different colours. On one set they write the verbs that are used to form phrasal verbs, on the other set they write prepositions. Then they shuffle the cards, take one card from each set, and decide whether such a phrasal verb exists and what it means. The game can be played by one person or in a group, either inside or outside the classroom.

VARIATION 4

Students choose three or four of the phrasal verbs they have checked in the dictionaries and write a short sketch or story which contains the ideas expressed by those verbs. For example, if the students suggest the phrasal verb _come into_, the sketch might include a reference to someone inheriting money. In the text there will not be a phrase that directly replaces the phrasal verb, the idea is simply referred to. The students read out their story or perform the sketch and the other groups suggest what the 'hidden' phrasal verbs are.

REMARKS

1 This may seem a rather mechanical approach to phrasal verbs, since the starting point is the formation of verbs and not the meaning. As a revision exercise, however, this shift in perspective can be useful. It also encourages learners to predict possible phrasal verbs and speculate about their meaning.

2 At some stage it may be necessary to point out the difference between prepositional verbs and phrasal verbs, for example, between *put up your hands* and *put up a visitor for the night*. In the first example there is a verb plus preposition but the normal meaning of *put* does not change. In the second the meaning of the expression can not be guessed from the verb alone. This activity focuses on the latter type of verb.

3 In stage 7, when using the phrasal verbs in context, learners are given an opportunity to check if their understanding of the phrasal verb and its use is correct.

2.7 The merry alphabet

LEVEL

Lower-intermediate and above

TIME

45 minutes

LANGUAGE

Vocabulary activation and expansion

PROCEDURE

1 In pairs or groups of three, learners write the English alphabet in a column in block capitals:
A
B
C
D
E . . .

2 Then they write one or more sentences with the first word beginning with the letter A, the second with the letter B, the third with the letter C and so on, for example: *A beast can drink even from glasses hanging in jail. Kim likes my new original piggy queen. Rolling Stones travelled under very wild Xmas yellow Zeppelin.*

3 Tell them not to worry about articles but that they should punctuate.

4 One pair writes their sentence/s on the blackboard.

5 The other learners ask the writers questions to clarify ambiguities or to expand the story, for example (for the sentences given in stage 2):
How big was the beast?
Was the beast hanging or were the glasses hanging?
What is the difference between a Xmas Zeppelin and an Easter one?

What is the difference between an original piggy queen and a fake one?
Do you mean the group the Rolling Stones?
The writers improvise the answers.

6 The procedure is repeated with a few more sentences.

7 The remaining sentences circulate and learners 'correct' them by adding missing function words or articles.

SAMPLE PRODUCT

A black cat dies every Friday. Good husbands invite jealous kings. Loud monks need orange people. Quite rough sailors travel under very windy Xmas Yuletide zephyrs.

Angela Brown cooks dinner every Friday gaily hopping in Jane's kitchen, looking more nervous over proper quality rising steam touching unique vase with x-rayed yolk zone.

VARIATION 1

If the class is large, stages 4 and 5 can be done in subgroups consisting of three pairs.

VARIATION 2

In stage 1, supply dictionaries and allow learners to browse through them if they get stuck.

REMARKS

This is an amusing activity and although it starts off in a relatively mechanical way, in the end it leads to very creative use of language.

2.8 What shall we eat?

LEVEL

Lower-intermediate and above

TIME

45–60 minutes

LANGUAGE

Names of food products, giving instructions

PROCEDURE

1 Learners try to remember what they ate and drank over the weekend.

2 Each student writes down this information in terms of the constituent ingredients, for example, they do not write *cake*, they write *sugar*, *flour*, *eggs*, and so on. They can ask the teacher for words and in a monolingual group there may be an element of translation at this stage.

3 Write on the board the following categories: meat, dairy products, cereals, vegetables, fats, spices, drinks, others.

4 Learners come to the board and write their ingredients under the appropriate headings. As they write, they should check what others have written in order to avoid repetition.

5 Go through the lists explaining words where necessary (or ask learners to). Erase any remaining repetitions and remove words which do not belong, such as *cake*.

6 Give the learners some time to copy vocabulary from the board.

7 Working in groups of three or four the learners now plan meals (breakfast, lunch, tea, and dinner) for favourite guests who will be visiting for a day. The dishes should be 'special' but they can only use the products from the list. That is all they have in the fridge or pantry.

8 The group writes out the menu with the names of the dishes. The menus are displayed on the wall or on a table.

9 Everyone mills around and puts on each menu a cross against something they would particularly like to eat. Each student puts one cross on every menu.

10 The groups retrieve their menus and see which dish is the most popular on their list.

11 They write out the recipe for this dish.

12 The recipes are read out beginning with the words: *You wanted to eat . . . and here is how to make it.* Other learners may ask for clarification if they do not understand.

VARIATION

The procedure can be adapted for other topics, such as 'do it yourself'. Learners make a list of the tools and materials they have at home, and of things that need to be repaired. In groups they discuss whether they have the necessary equipment and expertise to carry out the repairs.

2.9 What's gone?

LEVEL	**Lower-intermediate and above**
TIME	**20–30 minutes**
LANGUAGE	**Names of everyday objects and raw materials**

PROCEDURE

1 Students get into small groups and think of a popular raw material. They do not reveal this to the other groups.

2 Tell them that all of a sudden, for unknown reasons, this raw material has disappeared and so has everything made from it.

3 On a slip of paper students have to write six to eight short statements describing the consequences, for example, if 'wood' were the vanished raw material, the consequences would be: *Parts of some buildings have collapsed, I cannot show my homework to the teacher, I sleep on the floor.*

4 The lists are passed on from group to group and each group has to identify the raw material.

5 Discuss as a group which raw material was the most difficult one to identify and why.

VARIATION

Elicit from learners all the types of materials used for making clothing. Write the names on the blackboard. Allocate one material to each group of students. Make sure no group knows what the other groups have. Students then have to decide what clothes they would be left wearing if this material disappeared at this very moment. Students stand up and in turn tell the whole class what they would be wearing. The class has to decide what the material is.

2.10 Five favourite words

LEVEL	**All levels**
TIME	**25–30 minutes** (depending on size of class)
LANGUAGE	**Revising vocabulary**

PROCEDURE

1 Students look through their exercise books and select from the words that they have recently learned five words that they particularly like. They write these down.

2 Then they form pairs.

3 Together they negotiate a common list of five words from the ten they had originally. They can use whatever criteria they like to argue for or against words. It might be the shape, sound, association, or relevance of the word for them.

4 They write this new list on a separate piece of paper.

5 Collect the pieces of paper and redistribute them so that each pair receives a different list.

6 The pairs now write a dialogue or short story incorporating the words on the list they have just received.

7 Students read out their dialogues or stories and the others, with the exception of the authors of the list on which it was based, try to guess what the five listed words were.

REMARKS

The preparatory stages of the activity encourage the students to be selective in dealing with new vocabulary, while 'defending' their own words can help fix these in their memories. The random nature of the lists can make for some very memorable texts, which also helps with the acquisition of vocabulary.

3 Integrated skills

Introduction

Integrated skills activities, by definition, aim at improving the learners' general competence in the target language. Although a particular language focus is mentioned in the description of the activities, they all contain elements of the four basic skills: reading, writing, listening, and speaking. In the activities the skills are integrated within one topic. All the tasks therefore are strictly interdependent. For example, a text is written to be read by somebody else and to be retold later.

In this type of activity the teacher acts as an organizer and facilitator. The activities on the whole are fairly complex and intricate, and the success of one element depends on the success of the preceding one. Teachers must therefore constantly monitor and check the progress of the activities. In other words they cannot become members of a group to the same extent as in other types of activities. In some activities, however, there is a special role for teachers which allows them to take part while still controlling the activity (see 3.1).

3.1 *The Daily Gutter*

LEVEL	**Upper-intermediate and above**
TIME	**60–75 minutes**
LANGUAGE	**Language of discussion and interviews**
PROCEDURE	1 In pairs the learners take turns to talk about themselves, but everything they say must be a lie. They should try to be consistent. As they talk their partners may ask them questions but the answers must also be untrue. In this way they gradually build up a new persona or role for themselves. They should give their new persona a name.

2 Keeping in mind their new persona, they write down three topics they would be prepared to talk about (within the new role).

3 The learners now form new pairs and each person selects one of their partner's topics and interviews them about it as a reporter for the popular press. They take it in turns to interview each other and take notes.

4 Call and lead an editorial meeting for *The Daily Gutter*, a popular newspaper, inviting the 'reporters' to submit their stories for comment. Each pair can suggest one of their stories. You as the 'editor', or the group as a whole, can suggest amendments which could be made to give the story more of the flavour of a popular newspaper.

5 Learners in pairs write their articles to a deadline.

6 The finished articles are read out to the editorial group as a whole, who decide whether the stories can be printed as they stand, or if not, what amendments are required. They also decide which page they should appear on.

7 Put the stories up on the wall for the class to read, or if possible, type them up and make them into a class newspaper.

SAMPLE PRODUCT

RATS DINE ON LITERATURE-HUNGRY GIRL

The owner of a private home, James Bond, was horrified to find a mutilated body in his cellar. The victim, Sheila Goodpupil, 16, was found clutching a copy of *The Daily Gutter* in her blood-covered hand. She had obviously been looking for some good literature in the cellar. Relishing *The Daily Gutter* articles, she was attacked by a pack of hungry rats who ripped her throat out. Sheila Goodpupil was awarded this week's *The Daily Gutter* special badge.

VARIATION

You can introduce an additional stage between 4 and 5. Distribute real articles from the popular press and give learners time to look at the language used and the way the information is structured (but see Remarks below).

REMARKS

1 This activity can be done as part of a project on newspapers where learners have already had the opportunity to look at popular British newspapers or, if similar popular newspapers or magazines exist in the learners' own country, it may be sufficient to quickly remind them of the kind of language used there and then allow them to use a bilingual dictionary to find equivalent expressions.

2 The 'role' of interviewees here is not one that is imposed, or that needs to be remembered, but one that is developed spontaneously by the learners themselves.

3.2 Start your own business

LEVEL Intermediate and above

TIME 50–60 minutes

LANGUAGE Talking about skills, language of advertising

PROCEDURE 1 Learners individually make a list of twenty things they are good at, for example, *driving a car, writing letters, making excuses, dreaming*, and so on.

2 They get into pairs and in turn read out their lists. They tick the skills they share. If they realize that they have a skill which their partner listed but they forgot, they can add it to their lists.

3 Two pairs come together to form a group of four. They read out the skills that have been ticked and decide which skills all four have in common. The groups then go through these and choose skills which could be of interest or use to the general public. They also have to think of how these skills can become services. For example if *cooking* is a common skill, the services could be *open a snackbar, deliver pizzas to homes*, and so on.

4 Tell the groups that they have just established a 'Co-operative Business Venture' offering their services to the public. In order to hit the market and get publicity they must produce a brochure for their cooperative.

5 When they have finished, the groups display or read out the brochures. The entire class decides on:
– which business is the most and which the least financially viable
– which would win the most customers
– which would go bankrupt the soonest.
The learners themselves can decide on other criteria for evaluation.

SAMPLE PRODUCT

Are you overworked? Depressed? Do you feel like the slave of the Universe? We are here to help you. Just call or write to 'Home, Sweet Home' Ltd. and our agent will arrange everything for you.

- decorate and redecorate your flat (you will not be able to recognize it)
- do emergency baby-sitting
- do highly-qualified shopping and queuing
- letter writing (from business to love letters)

- scrub your flat clean
- provide cooking assistance (how to make ready-made food look home made)
- discover your artistic ego: water-colour and knitting courses

Once you've tried our service you'll never regret it, you'll never forget it.
'Home Sweet Home' Ltd. Best today, even better tomorrow!

Press the Button Society

Press the button 112
Everything is done for you
Are you lazy
I am too
Join me then
Let dreams come true

Press the button 112
Everything is done for you
We are lazy
Don't deny
There's no reason to be shy

Press the button 112
Everything is done for you
Your life will be laid with flowers
Once your wish is ours

For a mere
100 bucks a year
You'll have
Everything here
Without getting
Off your chair

Press the button 112
Everything is done for you
5-minute session
On the phone
All your depression
Forever gone.

Press here 112

REMARKS

First thing in the morning during an English class it may not be that easy to think of twenty things you are good at, but giving learners a fixed and relatively high number can mean that they come up with increasingly imaginative entries and that the services provided by the cooperatives can be quite varied.

3.3 Draw the simple present

LEVEL

Lower-intermediate

TIME

30–40 minutes

LANGUAGE

Names of objects, spatial prepositions, simple present

PROCEDURE

1 Tell the group that they are going to draw someone's living-room on the board. Invite a student to do the drawing or be prepared to do it yourself.

2 Invite suggestions from the class which the volunteer will draw on the board according to their instructions, for example, *There is a big armchair under the painting*; *There is an empty bottle lying by the coffee table*.

3 As more objects are added there will be more discussion of whether they are compatible, and of the character of the person who lives there. If the discussion is slow you can prompt it by asking questions, such as: *Does a man live here? Is he married? How old is he? What does he do? Does he read a lot? What sports does he play?*

4 Groups can then write a description of the person living in the room.

5 The stories are then read out, or displayed for the class to read.

VARIATION 1

The drawing can be done in smaller sub-groups, either on small blackboards or on large sheets of paper. When these are ready they can be passed on to other groups as the basis for further work as in stage 4 and 5. When the descriptions are finished groups can try to identify their own picture.

VARIATION 2

As an alternative to stage 4 the learners could write a story explaining why the room is now empty.

VARIATION 3

A third possibility at stage 4 could be for students to write a given number of sentences about the person living in the room, half with the simple present and the rest with the present progressive.

VARIATION 4 Instead of drawing a living room, students could draw the inside of a wardrobe or bathroom cabinet, the top of a desk or table, or the contents of a handbag or suitcase, for example.

VARIATION 5 Once the picture has been built up it can also be used to practise the contrast between the simple present and present progressive, for example: *What's she doing now? Well, she's probably not playing tennis because her racquet's behind the door.*

REMARKS With more advanced groups the activity can go on to stimulate a wide range of language, such as speculating, for example: *He might have lost a lot of money on the stock market.* Building up the character can lead into imaginative story-telling.

3.4 Invent your own country

LEVEL Lower-intermediate and above

TIME 40–60 minutes

LANGUAGE Revision of simple present, simple past, and present perfect

PROCEDURE 1 Give out small pieces of paper and pins, one to each person.

2 Everyone writes the name of a country and sticks or pins the paper on someone else's back. You should also have a piece of paper on your back.

3 In pairs, the learners ask each other questions to find out which country they are, for example, *Is my country rich or poor? Is the weather hot?* As pairs finish they can join others who are still working and help with answers.

4 Elicit from the group the topics they asked about and write these on the board.

5 In pairs they invent a country and prepare a description of it using the topics on the board.

6 Put pairs together to form groups of four and tell them they have in fact been describing the same country, but at different times, now and twenty years ago.

7 The students compare the descriptions and decide which is now and which twenty years ago. They also think of a name for the country.

8 Each group now prepares a press statement relating how their country has changed over the last twenty years.

9 One representative from each group comes to a table at the front of the class for the press conference. In turn they read out their statements and invite and answer questions from the 'press corps', that is, the rest of the class.

VARIATION 1

With a large class, instead of making groups of four in stage 6, you can put three or even four pairs together. They decide on the order of development of the country and continue as in stages 7–9.

VARIATION 2

Instead of inventing a country, learners can invent their own planets. The only difference is the time gap between the different descriptions (see stage 6). This is likely to be thousands or even millions of years.

VARIATION 3

To finish, you can stick the names of the countries around the room and invite students to stand by the country they would like to live in.

REMARKS

In stage 7 the students have to use all the information and, if necessary, give an explanation. For example, if one of the topics in stage 4 was geography and the country was once an island but is now part of the mainland, this can produce some very imaginative explanations.

3.5 Robots

LEVEL

Lower-intermediate and above

TIME

20–30 minutes

LANGUAGE

Instructions and discussion

PROCEDURE

1 Students form groups of three or four.

2 Their task is to program a robot. They have to decide what the robot can do and what it cannot do. They can also decide on how to operate it, for example, whether it reacts to the human voice or whether it needs to be touched.

3 In their groups they decide on the parameters and operating principles and write these down on a piece of paper. They also decide on a name for their robot, which they write on the paper.

4 Collect the papers.

5 Form the students into new groups, so that in each group there is at least one representative from each original group. For example, if there were originally four groups of three people, there should now be three groups of four people (see Remarks below).

6 In the new groups there is now a testing period. Students take it in turns to be the robot they programmed in their original group. The other students in the new group give instructions and try to find out what the robot's program is. They have two minutes to test each robot.

7 Students return to their original group and discuss what the programs of the other robots are.

VARIATION

1 Bring a robot group to the front of the classroom and ask the other groups what they think the robot's program is.

2 Read out that robot's original program so that the others can check their speculations.

3 In turn bring out the other robot groups and repeat the last two stages.

SAMPLE PRODUCT

Robot name : Husband

This robot can do anything a typical husband can do. It can watch television, read books, sleep, eat and drink, and talk. It cannot do anything in the kitchen, like making meals and it cannot do any housework. It responds to oral instructions given politely, but only if they are accompanied by a pat on the head.

REMARKS

One way of regrouping (see stage 5) is to give each student in the original groups a number or letter. For example, if there are three groups with four students in each, give students within each group a letter from A to D. Then give the instruction, 'All A students over here, all B students over there . . .' and so on.

3.6 Job interviews

LEVEL

Intermediate

TIME

30 minutes

LANGUAGE

Curricula vitae (CVs), talking about qualifications, interviewing

PROCEDURE

1 Learners write down in random order a list of all the jobs they have ever done, paid or unpaid (see Remarks below).

2 They stand up and arrange themselves in a straight line according to the number of jobs they have done so that the person who has done the most will be at one end of the line, the person with the least at the other.

3 Students now pair off from opposite ends of the line. The idea is that in each pair there will be approximately the same total number of jobs and therefore the pair work should take the same time.

4 Students now exchange lists, and by asking each other questions should prepare a full CV for the other person, with dates, exact nature of work, name of the company, and so on.

5 Divide the class into groups of four or five. Explain that they are going to interview candidates for a job. Each group should choose two or three interviewers and two candidates. The candidates could be those with more job experience.

6 The interviewers decide what the job on offer is. It can be as exotic or as ordinary as they like. They explain it to the candidates.

7 The interviewers then take the CVs from the candidates and carry out the interview like a formal job interview. The candidates are not allowed to invent information about themselves, but they have to persuade the panel that their actual experience and qualities make them a suitable candidate for this job.

8 The panel consult and make their decision. At the same time the candidates also decide between themselves who is the stronger candidate. Interviewers and candidates compare decisions.

REMARKS
It might seem that this activity would work only with older students. However, many younger students, even those still at school, will have some 'work' experience, such as baby-sitting, washing cars, doing the shopping, delivering newspapers, being secretary of school clubs, voluntary work, etc.

3.7 School reports

LEVEL
Intermediate and above

TIME
30–40 minutes

LANGUAGE
Revision of functions, register

PROCEDURE
1 Pair students off and have them remember their school years, or if still at school, their previous term or year. What subjects were they good at, what problems did they have, which subjects did they dislike? Students take it in turns to remember.

2 When all the students have finished, remind them of the format of an English school report, in other words of rubrics like *name, subject, grade, comment, general remarks.*

3 Individually students write a school report for their partners, basing it on what they have just heard. Make it clear that they may not be able to complete all the sections of the report from what they have been told, and that they may use their imagination to fill in the rest.

4 When the reports are ready, students fold them and give them to their partners with the instruction that they must not read them.

5 Students find other partners and exchange the reports.

6 They read the reports. In pairs they take it in turns to be 'parents' and talk to their 'children' about the report, praising, criticizing, and commenting. The 'children' may defend themselves, deny, argue, or make excuses.

SAMPLE PRODUCT

Name: *Jacek*

Subject	Grade	Comment
ENGLISH	5	*Very able, especially good at writing. Good at grammar.*
MATHEMATICS	4	*Good at tests, very interested in the subject.*
BIOLOGY	3	*Good at some parts; there are parts he knows less well.*
CHEMISTRY	5	*Extremely good, very enthusiastic.*
HISTORY	3	*Able, but indifferent.*
GEOGRAPHY	4	*Tends to quarrel with the teacher.*

General remarks

The problem, it appears, results from lack of ambition. He is likely to get 'O.' level.

REMARKS

1 In stage 2 students have to make the transfer from informal memories to formal report. As students begin writing, look at their work and point out mistakes of register.

2 As the students write the school reports they are not only using information given by their partner, but are also adding from their imagination. This added information means that the 'children' are more likely to disagree with the report and the conversation with their 'parent' will be more lively.

3 The activity is best suited for an even number of students in a class. If there is an odd number you could join in the activity yourself.

3.8 Holiday precautions

LEVEL

Intermediate and above

TIME

30 minutes

LANGUAGE

Giving warnings, stating precautions

PROCEDURE

1 Learners close their eyes and recall a favourite holiday through their five senses: the smells, the sounds, and so on.

2 They get into groups according to the location of their holidays: at the seaside, in the mountains, in the countryside, in the city, etc.

3 In their holiday groups they decide on and write down six necessary conditions for a perfect holiday in such a location. For example, a holiday in the mountains may require: *dry snow, no ice, blue skies, good boots, sunglasses, companions whose skiing is more or less at the same level*. Each student in the group should write these down.

4 Learners now pair off with a member of another group and exchange papers.

5 They take it in turns to point out the possible dangers or pitfalls of their partner's holiday, using their 'necessary conditions' as a guide. The other person has to suggest precautions they would take to avoid these problems. For example: *What if you break a leg while you're skiing?—I'll make sure I have full insurance before I go.*

6 If the precaution suggested is accepted as valid, the holidaymaker gets a point. If they cannot think of anything, or if the precaution is not accepted, the person suggesting the danger gets a point. If they cannot agree they should make a note of the problem. The person with more points at the end is the winner.

7 Any unresolved problems from stage 6 can be discussed by the whole group, with other precautions being suggested.

VARIATION

This activity can be used as a more controlled grammar exercise by giving students a model before they start stage 5. For example, you could tell them to make exchanges using first conditionals: *What will you do if the snow is horrible and wet? — No problem, I'll take lots of different waxes with me.*

3.9 Do you recognize your home?

LEVEL

Lower-intermediate and above

TIME

20–30 minutes

LANGUAGE

Describing homes

PROCEDURE

1 Learners pair off and in turns describe, honestly, their own home while their partner makes notes.

2 Taking the notes of their original partner's home with them, they form new pairs.

3 Each pair selects *one* of the two sets of notes they have
between them and writes a paragraph describing the property in
as glowing terms as possible, as if they were estate agents trying
to sell it. They should use all of the information from the notes,
but present it all positively. The property has *no* disadvantages!

4 Collect the completed descriptions from the pairs.

5 Read out the descriptions or display them for the students to
read. The owners try to recognize their own home.

3.10 Arguments

LEVEL

Intermediate and above

TIME

40–75 minutes

LANGUAGE

Language of discussion, putting forward arguments

PROCEDURE

1 Divide the class into two even groups and give the topic of the
discussion, for example 'Should prisons be abolished?'

2 Group A thinks of arguments for prisons and group B thinks
of arguments against prisons. Each member of the group should
write down all the arguments that come up in the discussion.

3 When each group has six or seven arguments, bring everyone
together again.

4 Elicit ways of disagreeing and introducing counter-arguments,
for example, *That's all very well, but what about . . .?*; *I am not
sure I would agree with that*; *Don't you think . . .?* If necessary
suggest some other ways yourself, and write all of these on the
board.

5 Pair off learners in such a way that each pair consists of a
student from group A and one from group B. They should sit
facing each other, preferably across the table.

6 Tell them they will have a table tennis match, playing with
arguments instead of a ball. The subject is: *Should prisons be
abolished?* (for example). The rules are as follows: Student A puts
forward one argument from their list and student B counters
with an argument from their own list. The argument may be
related to the preceding argument of the opponent, but does not
have to be. They choose the arguments from their own lists in
any order, and expressions for the language of discussion from
the board. The pairs should work simultaneously.

7 When you see that the students have used up all the
arguments from their lists, do not tell them that the activity is
over. Allow a free discussion to develop.

8 If a pair finishes earlier, ask them to reflect on their discussion. They can exchange their lists of arguments and decide which were the strongest and which were the weakest arguments of their opponent. They can then rank them.

SAMPLE PRODUCT

Arguments for:

1. A good way to punish is to limit freedom.
2. Keeps down the number of criminals running about.
3. Cheap labour force.
4. Nothing better has been invented.
5. All arguments against prison are arguments against conditions in prison.
6. Potential criminals are afraid of prisons.
7. Prisons offer a possibility of getting an education.

Arguments against:

1. Bad influence on young offenders from notorious criminals: learning bad habits from other inmates.
2. Prisons are ineffective.
3. Deprivation in prison.
4. Guards are sadistic.
5. Mixing of petty offenders with serious criminals.
6. Bad effect on health.
7. When they leave prison, ex-prisoners need rehabilitation and resocialization.

VARIATION   This activity is adaptable for any argumentative topic.

REMARKS   1 This is a very good introductory exercise for free discussions. Students learn to discuss and parry arguments but do not feel personally responsible for them. They do not feel personally threatened by having to convince the opponent, and therefore are more relaxed. They can play more with the language and juggle with the arguments because they realize that this is just a game.

2 This activity can be extended to include other skills, for example by using the discussion as a preparation for writing an argumentative essay.

4 Writing

Introduction

In these activities writing is never carried out in isolation. Rather it is the main focus in an integrated and interdependent activity. The introductory phase provides a springboard for the writing, which in turn serves as the basis for subsequent activities. The writing itself is characterized by the following features:

– The writing task is done for a purpose: we write because we want to inform, or request information, because we want something done, or because we want to amuse, for example.

– The writer knows that what is written will be read and knows who the audience will be.

– The audience in this case is not the teacher and the reason for writing and reading is not for assessment or correction.

– The readers will be reading attentively and purposefully because they will be required to react to the text, and to do something with it.

These characteristics make for greater authenticity of tasks in the writing lesson. As the writing is part of an integrated set of tasks it is possible to say whether the writers have been successful, and have achieved their goal. The main emphasis in these activities is the successful completion of the writing task as the basis for subsequent work, rather than the provision of linguistic forms which the learner is required simply to incorporate into the text. There are no prescribed models, and the learners' language is moulded to fit what they want to say rather than their thoughts being constricted by the language provided.

Teachers, as *participants* in the activity, are free to introduce into their own texts any aspect of language which they consider may be useful to the learners, and which will be available to learners in the next stages of the lesson. At the same time, while learners are writing, the teacher can give immediate help with vocabulary, grammar, and phrasing.

It is for the teacher to decide at what point the texts will be corrected, in what way, and by whom (the teacher or other learners). However, since this is an integrated writing activity where the writer has to write clearly, effectively, and unambiguously in order to facilitate further stages of the lesson, the teacher may prefer not to interrupt the flow of the lesson by distracting learners' attention from meaning to form. It may be preferable to leave correction, of whatever kind, until later.

4.1 Dictionary of . . .

LEVEL

Lower-intermediate and above

TIME

30–60 minutes

LANGUAGE

Topic vocabulary expansion, definitions, and dictionary entries

PROCEDURE

1 Learners work in five small groups. They write down the English alphabet vertically, one letter on each or every other line. Assign to each group a part of the alphabet: A–E, F–J, for example, or even better, jumbled-up letters to avoid a group getting the difficult combination VWXYZ.

2 The letters provide the frame: the first letters of words which, according to learners, should be found in a Dictionary of a particular subject—for example Horror. They first write the word, then next to it a short definition explaining the meaning of the word, for example:
A — agony — the last painful moments of life.
B — blood-drinker — a vampire who prefers blood to red wine.
If the learners cannot think of a word beginning with a certain letter they can browse through a monolingual dictionary looking for a word that could qualify or be adapted as an entry in the Dictionary of Horror, for example:
Z — ? — zoom — the noise you make when you run away from a ghost.

3 Give out small slips of paper.

4 Students copy out the headings and the definitions so that each is on a separate slip, i.e. on one slip there is either a heading or a definition.

5 The sets are then passed on to other groups. Each group has to reassemble the slips, matching headings with definitions.

6 They copy out the full entries and then pass the slips on, jumbled up again.

7 The group as a whole can suggest other entries or definitions which in their opinion should be incorporated into the Dictionary.

VARIATION 1

In pairs or small groups, learners can be assigned the whole alphabet and write all the entries. They cut up their dictionaries into the different entries, with title and description remaining on the same piece of paper. The class as a whole now amalgamates all the entries into one common dictionary in the correct alphabetical order under each letter, writing them neatly, and perhaps illustrating them. The dictionary is then exhibited on the wall. If suitable facilities are available, you can photocopy individual copies for learners to keep.

SAMPLE PRODUCT   **Extracts from two Dictionaries of Laziness:**

Armchair	the only chair you can accept
Bachelor	a man too lazy to take pains to get married
Cat	an animal that sets a good example of taking naps
Dandelion	a very passive lion indeed
Elbow	means of supporting a relaxing body
Feet	very sensitive parts of the human body which need long bathing in hot water with mustard. They also lend themselves to skilful and careful powdering.
Green apple	an apple which refuses to ripen (too much effort)

Quicksilver	metal that is never lazy
Runner	a person too lazy to stop running
Sandwich	something a lazy cook could make for dinner.
Telepathy	a technique of communication a sloth would employ to avoid walking to the phone book.
Unicorn	an animal too lazy to carry two horns.
Vanish	to disappear when asked to do something
Widow	a woman too lazy to remarry
X	a letter too lazy to begin many English words.
Yeti	an animal too lazy to introduce itself.
Zebra	an animal too lazy to take off its pyjamas.

VARIATION 2   If the class is big, divide students into two big groups and then divide these groups into five sub-groups. The activity then runs simultaneously in both groups and for each the procedure is as described above. Then the whole class is brought together again and the learners compile one dictionary from the two versions, put all the entries together in correct alphabetical order, write them out neatly, and perhaps illustrate them. The dictionary can later be exhibited or photocopied for everyone to keep.

REMARKS   This activity encourages learners to look through monolingual dictionaries and to read the entries purposefully. It also gives learners an opportunity to be creative, and to play with words, trying to invent their own new meanings, for example:
X — X — the shape your legs take when you see a vampire.
Y — YGCA — Young Ghosts' Christian Association.

4.2 The shortest review

LEVEL   **Intermediate and above**

TIME   **45 minutes**

LANGUAGE   **Organization of a paragraph, linking words, paraphrasing**

PROCEDURE   **1** In pairs learners prepare a list of titles of the following: a film, a book, a TV series, a play, musical, or other cultural event, a record, a coursebook. Both people should have seen, read, or heard these items and expect other people in the class to know them as well.

2 All the learners mill around and look at the lists. The class then decides on *one* common title to work on. They must reach agreement. Explain that they do not have to like the title—the review can be negative.

3 Individually learners then write a one-sentence review of whatever it is the class have chosen.

4 Stand at the board. Learners who are ready come up to you with their sentence. Check the sentence. Let the learners write their own sentences on the board.

5 When all the sentences are on the board (have a maximum of ten), ask all the learners together to read them out loud. As they do this, number the sentences.

6 The task of the learners now is to combine the sentences on the board into a one- or two-paragraph review. They can introduce any changes they like to improve the paragraph, such as adding linking words, omitting words, and making stylistic modifications. You may first need to demonstrate the task on two sentences on the board, and revise the linking words and phrases already known to the learners.

7 Learners get into pairs and start carrying out the task by carefully re-reading the sentences and noting down their proposed sequence for the paragraph. This is when the numbers are helpful.

8 When the sequence has been agreed, learners write the reviews, one per pair. You should assist them in their work.

9 When all the versions of the review are ready, they are circulated and each learner reads them, paying attention to four areas:

– how all the sentences have been combined

– how the particular review compares with their own review

– if their own sentence has been incorporated and whether it has been changed

– possible mistakes.

10 Learners discuss their doubts and problems with particular sentences. They can nominate an 'enfant terrible', i.e. the sentence which caused the most problems.

SAMPLE PRODUCT   Here are two reviews of the film *Fiddler on the Roof*, written using the same sentences from stage 5. They show how the same sentences can be combined in quite different ways to produce different texts.

First review

This film tells us about the life of a Jewish milkman and his family showing the customs and living conditions of the Russian Jews before the First World War. One of the aspects is the problem of male domination in the family which is very interesting but sometimes a little bit funny, e.g. when Teve decided to see Motel's new sewing machine. There is also a very beautiful presentation of old Jewish customs like a wedding ceremony and the bottle dance. It is an extraordinary film with beautiful and enjoyable songs full of wonderful music and specific Jewish sense of humour. No wonder that after the film everyone who has seen it sings 'If I were a rich man'. Other memorable features of the film were the performance of the actor who played Topol, the main character, really remarkably and extremely well, and the uniformly high quality of the songs both in terms of the lyrics and the melodies which made the film quite unforgettable.

Second review

'Fiddler on the Roof' is an extraordinary film with beautiful songs full of music and a specific Jewish sense of humour. The film tells of the life of a Jewish milkman and his family, showing the customs and living conditions of the Russian Jews before the First World War. The main character was really remarkable and was extremely well acted. The most memorable feature of the film was indeed the performance of Topol, and the uniformly high quality of the songs both in terms of the lyrics and the melodies.

I enjoyed very much the songs and beautiful presentation of old Jewish customs like the wedding ceremony or the bottle dance. I also found the problem of male domination in the family very interesting but sometimes a little bit funny, for example, when Teve decided to see Motel's new sewing machine. However, the music is most important because days after the film everyone who has seen it sings 'If I were a rich man...'.

VARIATION 1   If most of the reviews were favourable, learners can be asked to continue their reviews, by writing another, unfavourable paragraph which would concentrate on the weak points. By the time they write a second paragraph, they are generally more conscious of the linking words and structure.

VARIATION 2   Learners could write one-sentence reviews of the coursebook they are or have been using. If they are using two coursebooks at the same time, or had earlier used another one in the same group, they can compare the two. Preferably this activity should be used towards the end of the course. It is a good feedback session on what the learners' expectations are in terms of coursebooks.

SAMPLE PRODUCT   Learners were writing a review of the coursebook they were using. The titles of the books have been replaced by 'X' and 'Y'.

SENTENCES

1 The book gives the possibility to learn vocabulary which you can meet in everyday life, life with its different problems.
2 To me, this book appears to be much easier than the one which we had last year.
3 This book is written to prepare you for a specific exam.
4 The material given in the book: grammar, new words, new ideas, is presented in a very attractive way.
5 X, an English coursebook, is a modern, interestingly arranged book with good grammar exercises.
6 X gives in an attractive way a variety of topics connected with everyday life.
7 The book has a very interesting form and has both lots of new information and revises some already known grammar structures.
8 I found the book interesting, touching many aspects of life, but surprisingly I regard it as easier than Y which we had last year.

REVIEW

X, an English coursebook, is a modern, interestingly arranged book with good grammar exercises. It gives in an attractive way a variety of topics and the possibility of learning vocabulary which you can meet in everyday life, life with its different problems. This book is written to prepare you for a specific exam. The material given: grammar, new words, and new ideas, is presented in a very attractive form. It has a very interesting structure and has both lots of new information and revises some already known grammar. To me, this book appears to be much easier than the one which we had last year. Of course, I found it quite interesting and it touched on many aspects of life, but as I mentioned above I regard it as easier than Y.

REMARKS

1 If the class is large, for example twenty to forty learners, you should divide them into groups of ten, as more than ten sentences may make for an unmanageably long paragraph, and in stage 4, instead of writing on the board, learners dictate their sentences to the rest of their group, after the teacher has checked them for correctness. In stage 9 they circulate the reviews within their group.

2 Even when a number of students come up with very similar sentences they can still link them in a natural way by paraphrasing, emphasizing, or using repetition. For example: *It's an excellent book* and *It's a fantastic book* can be linked in this way: *This is an excellent book. Indeed, I would even go so far as to say it is a truly fantastic book.*

4.3 What would you like to know?

LEVEL

Lower-intermediate and above

TIME

60–90 minutes

LANGUAGE

Organizing information

PROCEDURE

1 Learners sit in a large circle or in any other way which will allow the smooth circulation of sheets of paper.

2 Give each student a sheet of paper. They write the main topic of their interests at the top of the page. Adults can briefly describe their profession, or if the learners are school students or all have the same profession, use hobbies.

3 Each student passes the sheet to the person on the left, who reads the title and writes a question about the subject. The papers are passed on again to the left.

4 The procedure is repeated with learners writing a question on every piece of paper they receive. They should read the questions that have already been written, so as to avoid repetition.

5 When the papers have come back to their owners they read all the questions and then write a text which answers them. They decide on the order in which they will answer the questions and on how to organize the text, but they must answer *all* the questions.

6 The questions and the corresponding texts are displayed together and learners mill around reading the questions and responses, checking if their question has been answered. If the learners have any queries about the way their questions were answered they should make a note of these.

7 In turn, the writers of the texts stand by their work while the other members of the group ask for clarification, or for an answer if their question was not answered in the text.

SAMPLE PRODUCT

```
TOPIC

I deal with the problem of how to make people want to listen to the radio.
The way the news is read and how to pronounce words correctly is important.

QUESTIONS

Are you a radio announcer?
Can you in any way influence the news you read?
What is correct pronunciation?
How many ways can the news be read?
For how many hours can you read the news without a break?
What kind of news do you read?
Are you a psychologist?
Have you the best pronunciation?
And what about keeping smiling?
Is it possible for you to deal a bit with the problem of how to make people
learn English successfully?
What made you deal with a problem like that?

RESPONSE TEXT

I'm not the best of the announcers at pronunciation. The correct
pronunciation is the way you speak the words: clearly, with correct accent
and whole text according to the melody of the language, not staccato for
instance. It's possible to give your influence, or show your attitude to
the news you read. So you can read the news in many ways. Most information
you read seriously but generally you keep in your mind the idea 'keep
smiling'. You try to get attention from the listeners. For me what I read
is always more important than the form. I can't read for hours without a
break - I think about one hour is my limit.
```

VARIATION 1   If the class is too big, divide the learners into smaller subgroups of about ten to twelve, and continue as above.

VARIATION 2   In stage 6 it is also possible to jumble up the sheets with questions and responses, label them 1,2,3 . . . and a,b,c . . . at random, and learners have to match them into pairs while reading.

REMARKS   1 Teachers can also join in with this activity, asking questions and writing responses to questions addressed to them.

2 The way the activity is structured ensures that the information the author includes in the text is information required by particular members of the group. Everyone therefore has a reason for writing and reading the texts.

3 This activity is a real test of learners' abilities to communicate in writing. They must phrase their questions correctly and clearly if they want to be understood. That is why the questions are not corrected by the teacher. Equally there is no correction of the texts so the writers have to make sure that they answer all the questions fully and clearly. Learners themselves realize whether they have successfully communicated or not by the further questions that are asked in stage 7. This stage also offers a safety net which gives learners an opportunity to sort out ambiguities and to get the answers they wanted.

4.4 What's the news today?

LEVEL

Intermediate and above

TIME

45–60 minutes

LANGUAGE

Language of headlines, expressing attitudes

PROCEDURE

1 Choose a very recent event in politics or current affairs that affects everybody in the class in some way.

2 Ask each student to write the kind of headline on the event that they would expect to find in a daily newspaper. Some old English-language newspapers could be displayed at this point, if they are available.

3 Check that the headlines are grammatically correct. Learners write them up on the board (see examples below).

4 Discuss the headlines briefly. Learners should decide whether all the headlines express the same tone, mood, and attitude.

5 On slips of paper learners, individually, write two to three words that in their opinion describe the main attitude expressed in all the headlines.

6 Learners form pairs and explain to their partners why they chose these words and why they think they are suitable and relevant.

7 They then write their words on the board. Eliminate repetitions.

8 The class together then write a newspaper article on the issue, incorporating the words from the board. However, they do not have to use the word in the precise form in which it was written. They can also build a word from it, for example, if the word was 'sorrow' they could also use 'sorrowful', 'sorry'.

9 Individual learners suggest possible sentences (less confident learners may need to be encouraged). The class discusses each in turn for appropriacy. As they agree on a sentence they write it on the board. They should also agree that it is grammatically correct. They continue until they have a complete and coherent article on the board.

SAMPLE PRODUCT   The issue the learners were working on was the first presidential election in post-war Poland. There were very mixed feelings about the event the following day, which was the day the class was held.

HEADLINES   WORDS DESCRIBING ATTITUDE

Incredible choice of Jaruzelski   surprise   disappointment
No chance of big changes   resignation   doubt
The most exciting election   impatience   irony
  in post-war times   interesting   sorrow
The only choice?   commitment   disappointed
Is one vote really enough?   unhappy

ARTICLE PRODUCED BY THE GROUP
With interest and growing impatience did we observe the eagerly awaited presidential
election. It was amazing to observe anger, fear, and excitement on the faces of the
members of Parliament. We must agree that the criticism and irony of Michnik in his
speech show his big commitment to this event. Sorrow and disappointment were
expressed in the letters of the absent MPs. The doubts about the way of voting
showed some contradictions in the procedure. It showed the need for democracy and
the result of voting turned out to be a huge disillusionment and a great surprise.
The unhappy members of the opposition were full of resignation.

VARIATION 1   If the class is too big, divide learners into subgroups at stage 8 and continue the procedure.

VARIATION 2   To keep the article shorter, limit the number of words to *one* in stage 5.

REMARKS   **1** This activity is most successful when all learners are involved in the issue and when they have not yet read the news coverage, so that the group expresses its own opinions instead of simply repeating those of local journalists.

2 This activity is also useful in organizing activities around issues and events where no written English news coverage is available.

3 Usually learners want to have their own copy of this article, so make sure they have time to copy it from the board.

4.5 How much do we really know?

LEVEL　　　　　Intermediate and above

TIME　　　　　60–90 minutes

LANGUAGE　　　　　Organizing information

PROCEDURE　　　　　1 Divide the class into groups of four and ask them to recall everything they know about a current issue or event of your choice (or of theirs). All the groups use the same issue or event, for example an earthquake, election, or hijack.

2 As learners brainstorm, they make short notes of everything they remember.

3 As a group they write an article on the subject. They should decide first what aspect(s) of the problem they are going to consider, and whether their article will have a particular slant. They should also give it a title/headline. You should help them with any language problems and make sure the text is correct.

4 When the groups are ready the articles are circulated. In the articles they receive, each group is to look for:
- facts that they as a group did not remember
- ways of giving information or wording that they like or are new to them.

5 The class can decide which group has written the best article.

SAMPLE PRODUCT　　　　　The subject was the earthquake in Armenia which had happened three days before the lesson.

A terrible earthquake occurred in Armenia, one of the Soviet republics. According to recent information it took 60 thousand lives and brought about an enormous number of homeless people. It came in two waves, destroying two cities with most of the inhabitants buried in rubble.

　　When the news of the earthquake was broadcast to the world, international aid was organized: transports of food, medicines, and various equipment started to flow to Armenia. Rescue teams with specially-trained dogs are searching the rubble all the time for casualties trapped in it. Field hospitals are full of injured people and temporary housing is being organized for the homeless people.

　　The scale of the tragedy could have been lessened if building standards had been complied with. Moreover, this earthquake was not predicted by scientists, who admitted that they had no proper equipment to detect the coming of an earthquake. Furthermore, it was said on the radio that there was no connection between this earthquake and any underground nuclear explosion.

　　It is the worst earthquake in this region since the beginning of the century.

VARIATION　　　　　The subject of the activity can also be: *How much do we remember about . . .?* This may be topical on the anniversary of particular events, such as the tenth anniversary of John Lennon's assassination. Learners have to recall all the facts they can and write a suitable text, for example a commemorative article.

4.6 Whose life?

LEVEL

Intermediate and above

TIME

60 minutes

LANGUAGE

Writing biographies

PROCEDURE

1 Give each student a sheet of paper (A4 is ideal). Arrange the students in large circles of up to twenty.

2 They have to imagine the life story of a person born on a given date, for example 2nd January 1920. At the top of the sheet everybody writes: *2nd January 1920—born in. . . .* They complete the sentence individually, giving the place and family background, for example, *2nd January 1920—born in Krakow, Poland, in a well-to-do professional family.*

3 Each student folds the paper so that the first line cannot be read, and passes their sheet clockwise to the next student who continues writing the life story of the character they have in mind, but on somebody else's sheet.

4 After each entry the sheet is folded and passed on.

5 When the papers have almost come full circle, tell them that they will be able to write only two or three more entries and that they can now 'kill off' the character, if they wish.

6 When the circle is completed students unfold their sheet of paper and read what has happened to the character.

7 Learners individually skim through the texts and decide if the person is a man or a woman and invent a name.

8 Then the learners take another sheet of paper and write out in full the person's life story. They have to maintain the given sequence of events so they may have to find some clever ways of accounting for the unexpected twists in the person's life, for example, *1968—died in London, 1970—went to Paris.* One possible way of handling this is: *Many people thought that he died in 1968, but in fact he went to Paris under another name.*

9 As each life story is ready, display them on the wall for students to read while other people are finishing their writing.

REMARKS

This is a good exercise on the use of connectives and sequencing. It is usually very enjoyable because learners have to use their ingenuity in handling sometimes contradictory facts. They also practise the language of descriptions.

4.7 My great-, great-, great- . . .

LEVEL   Lower-intermediate and above

TIME   45–60 minutes

LANGUAGE   Describing people and past events

PROCEDURE   1 Learners individually recall the most remote ancestor they know anything about. They write down all the facts they remember.

2 In pairs they tell their partners what they can remember.

3 They decide which of the two people they have talked about they find more appealing.

4 Still in pairs, they discuss what else might have happened in the person's life, bearing in mind their background and status, the history of the country in which they lived, and the typical fates of people who lived at that time.

5 Then in pairs they write the life story of the person.

6 The texts are exhibited and learners mill around reading the stories.

7 Learners try to fit all the people described into one family tree and, as a whole group, invent a family saga. Use the floor to spread out the texts representing the particular people. A large space is useful for negotiations and rearrangement.

REMARKS   This activity starts with real data and then becomes a fully imaginative activity calling upon the learners' general historical and social knowledge.

4.8 The review of the decade

LEVEL   Intermediate and upwards

TIME   60–90 minutes

LANGUAGE   Negotiating, organizing information

PROCEDURE   1 Write on the board the years of the past decade, leaving spaces to write in information.

2 Learners recall what happened in the world, in their native country, and in their personal life, in particular years of the decade.

3 Call out the years and ask learners to suggest events. Write four or five events for each year on the board.

4 When all the years have been discussed learners get into groups of three or four.

5 In the groups they write a review of the decade, incorporating all the facts from the board and trying to find a central theme.

6 Collect and redistribute the reviews.

7 Groups read the reviews and choose criteria by which to edit them, for example age of the readers, type of newspaper, political opinion of the group.

8 They edit and rewrite the reviews, using these criteria.

9 The original reviews are displayed next to the edited versions. Students read both the texts and try to find out what the editing principles were.

10 Bring the students together. Students discuss what they think the editing principles for each text were. The editors say whether the other students have correctly identified them.

VARIATION

The same procedure can be applied to writing a review of the past year using months instead of years.

REMARKS

In stage 9 the interest tends to be high for two reasons: each group has worked with the same raw data but has probably handled it in quite a different way, and then the texts were edited according to different criteria. The reading stage is therefore very intensive.

4.9 Fictional agony column

LEVEL

Lower-intermediate and above

TIME

45 minutes

LANGUAGE

Describing problems, giving advice

PROCEDURE

1 Everyone writes down the titles of ten books and films they have read or seen.

2 People mill around, looking at each other's lists, and ask each new partner about *one* of the books or films they themselves have not read or seen.

3 The whole class finds one film or book that everyone has seen or read. (This may be a title that was not on anyone's original list.)

4 Ask the students to name a character who had a problem in that book/film, and as a class orally reconstruct the problem and what the character did about it. You should now explain what an agony column is.

5 Students look for a partner who has one title in common with them on their original list.

6 Students recall a character from this book/film who had a problem.

7 They write a letter from that character to an agony column, outlining the problem and asking for advice.

8 When the letters are written, circulate them around the class. Each pair writes one sentence giving advice to every character. The activity continues until the students get their own letters back and can read the advice.

9 Display the letters on the wall so that students have the chance to read all the advice that was given.

SAMPLE PRODUCT

Dear Agony Column Auntie,

I am a famous actor and everybody in the whole world knows me very well. But I am not a person without problems.

First of all I have very bad pronunciation. Even my youngest nephews play tricks on me. The way I look makes me very unhappy especially when I see my smile in the mirror. It is definitely too wide. What can I do? Can you help me?

Yours,

Donald Duck.

Dear Donald,

You sound a very sensitive and sensible person, and I am sure your situation is difficult.

I cannot give you any plain advice, but if I were you I would try not to smile at all or to change my teeth.

Or the best piece of advice is to have plastic surgery.

Yours,

Agony Column Auntie.

REMARKS

In stage 5 it is possible that not everyone will find a partner who has a title in common with them. Students without a partner should pair off and agree on a title from one of their lists or quickly find another book or film they have both read or seen.

4.10 Number poetry

LEVEL

Lower-intermediate and above

TIME

40 mintues

LANGUAGE

Playing with words

PROCEDURE

1 Divide the class into groups of ten people and assign everyone in the group a number from 0 to 9.

2 On a piece of paper, students write as many sentences as possible incorporating their number. There should be at least six sentences.
Examples:
Two is the perfect number.
I have two legs.
There are two sides to every coin.

3 Students pass their sentences around the group to the person on their left.

4 Repeat stage 3 twice. This ensures that when pairs are formed no-one will be working with their own sentences.

5 Students form pairs with the person next to them.

6 Working with the two sets of sentences they have between them, students write two verses of a poem: one for each number. They can alter the sequence of the sentences, delete or add words, or drop entire sentences if they wish.

7 When they have written their verses, give them a few minutes to practise reading them out loud.

8 Students read out their verses in numerical order, that is, the first will be the verse on '0', then '1', and so on.

REMARKS

It is not necessary to use all the numbers from 0 to 9. You can assign numbers to suit the size of the group. For example, if there are eighteen people you could divide them into groups of six and assign the numbers from 0 to 5.

5 Translation

Introduction

We are not advocating a wholesale return to translation as a method of learning and teaching languages. It can, however, serve as a way of identifying gaps in the learners' knowledge of the target language. Part of what learners bring into the classroom, clearly, is their knowledge of their first language and its culture. The activities here help the learners to bring these into their knowledge of the second language, offering them a chance to incorporate imagery from their own cultural background into the target language and so use it more vividly.

Through these translation activities the teacher can also be made aware of the source of some mistakes made when students translate literally from the native language.

The activities fall into two types:

– Those which encourage the learner to bring an example of their first language use into the classroom and then work on how to express this in English

– Activities which call on learners to dip into their collective cultural heritage in remembering fragments of songs, poems, or other literature which is familiar to them.

A characteristic of these activities is that the learners themselves have a choice of which text they work on, so that it is a text which has significance for them.

The activities have been used with monolingual groups, but many lend themselves to adaptation for multilingual groups, provided there are monolingual subgroups. In this case part of the activity can be carried out in monolingual subgroups and other parts in multilingual groups. For example, monolingual groups can prepare a first rough translation into English of a fragment of poetry. The multilingual groups can then work on a polished version.

The sample products given here do not include the stages that were written in the native language, only the English versions.

5.1 Telephone call

LEVEL

Lower-intermediate and above

TIME

30–40 minutes

LANGUAGE

Everyday exchanges

PROCEDURE

1 Learners sit back (if they wish they may close their eyes), and recall the last telephone conversation they had in their native language.

2 Everyone writes down their own conversations translated into English, asking you for help if necessary. The English translation should be as true as possible to the native-language original. The learners should underline in the text any problems they have had in translating particular words or phrases.

3 Learners then work in pairs and try to improve on the accuracy of their English versions.

4 The corrected end products are displayed for everyone to read. When they have read them, learners try to rank the conversations, arranging them according to a given criterion, such as 'most formal' to 'most informal', or according to a criterion suggested by the learners themselves.

SAMPLE PRODUCT

This was a telephone conversation 12-year-old Marta had with her friend Justyna.

— Hello!

— It's Justyna <u>on this side</u>. By the way, do you remember what exercises we had to do at home?

— Yes, I do. It was page 230, exercises 5, 6, 7.

— Thanks.

— Do you know, when I saw Aurelia today, I thought I would die!

— Yes, she had those terrible trousers ^{on} again!

— And I <u>could just</u> not look at her T-shirt.

— And those badges!

— She looked like a punk or <u>anything</u> like that!

— Yes, and her shoes.

— That colour did not match the trousers or anything.

— Yes, but you must understand she has no taste at all!

— But would you dress like that?

— No, certainly not.

— And Anna was looking horrible too.

— She has got no taste <u>too</u>!

REMARKS

1 If the group is monolingual, or if there are monolingual subgroups, the language work can continue on the underlined parts of the conversations. Learners in groups try to decide what were the native language equivalents of the troublesome lexis or structures. They translate the expressions or words back into the native language.

2 If you find out in the course of the lesson that the conversations produced are culturally or socially unacceptable in English, you can use the texts as the basis for further work.

3 In stage 2, the length of the conversation may depend on the level of the students. It might be a good idea to suggest a time limit of ten minutes for this writing stage.

4 In stage 4 the ranking is best displayed on the classroom wall, on the floor, or in the corridor outside the classroom. To be successful, this stage of the activity needs a lot of space.

5 This activity is very revealing as it can give you insight into the interests and world of the learners. The telephone conversation of a 12-year-old girl, for example, can be very different from that of a middle-aged businessman. It also reveals cultural differences in ways of talking on the phone, e.g. answering the phone, addressing people, and ending a conversation.

6 The activity also requires the learners to write down exchanges that are normally only spoken. In this way you can find mistakes that have not been corrected simply because they have not been heard. For example, some of our learners were saying *What's a pity!*, merging *What a pity* and *That's a pity*.

5.2 My favourite numbers and dates

LEVEL

Elementary

TIME

15–30 minutes

LANGUAGE

Numbers and dates, simple present and past

PROCEDURE

1 Learners write down on a separate piece of paper ten numbers or dates that are important to them. These can be of personal, historical, or social importance.

2 Collect the papers.

3 Read out a few numbers or dates at random.

4 Students who have written those numbers or dates raise their hands.

5 Redistribute the papers at random, making sure that no-one receives their own.

6 Students move around and try to find the owner by reading out, not showing, the dates and numbers they have received.

7 When students find the owner they give back the piece of paper. This stage continues until everyone has got their paper back.

8 Students form small groups of three or four and tell each other why the dates and numbers are important for them. Most of this will be in the native language. The group helps each person to translate this information into English and write a sentence beside each number or date.
Examples:
1984: My first child was born
711220: My Identity Card number

9 Collect the papers and write identifying letters on them, for example from A to P.

10 Fix them to the walls. Students read the information and note down who they think the papers belong to, for example 'Pawel—A'.

11 Ask the class as a whole who they think each paper belongs to. The real 'owner' can then stand up.

VARIATIONS

There are a number of variations on this activity, not necessarily requiring translation. For example, as a shorter activity learners can simply write the dates and numbers and then get into pairs and try to guess what these refer to. This can be done with all levels of students.

REMARKS

1 Teaching numbers and dates can often be very impersonal, whereas this activity introduces a strong personal element by giving learners an opportunity to say something meaningful about themselves. Most students will relish this, but some may find it embarrassing or even upsetting.

2 At its most simple this activity can be used as a listening recognition task.

5.3 My story?

LEVEL

Lower-intermediate and above

TIME

45–60 minutes

LANGUAGE

Giving the gist

PROCEDURE

1 Learners recall something really exciting that has happened to them or somebody in their family, or a particularly happy moment in their lives.

2 They describe this event in writing, in their own language, in a specified number of words. The stories should be written in a dramatic and gripping way.

3 Redistribute the texts and give each student five minutes to read the story and memorize it.

4 Collect the texts and ask each student to write in English the story they have just read, trying to preserve the character and drama of the original. You can make the original versions available on request for a short time, but the learners should not have them in front of them all the time.

5 Display all the stories. Learners mill around, read the stories, and look for their own.

6 Give out the native-language versions at random and ask learners to pair the originals with the translations.

7 Translators take the original version and their own translation and underline, in the original, phrases or words which they did not know, or would not know, how to translate. Discuss these with the whole class.

SAMPLE PRODUCT

> Marek is a doctor and works in the hospital. A few days ago, ~~he was a witness of~~
> witnessed the installation of
> ~~installing/~~a special kind of telephone in his hospital. It was connected with George
>   a
> Bush's visit to Gdansk. Using this telephone it was possible to get ~~/the~~ connection to
>   installed
> Washington in 3 seconds by satellite. This telephone was ~~/set~~ by a 16-year-old boy,
> who had a few technical problems, because of differences between Polish and
> American standards.

VARIATION

This can be a 'Chinese whispers-style' activity. Instead of writing the stories, learners tell them.

1 Learners sit in circles of ten to twelve (there must be an even number).

2 They form pairs. In each pair one person is A and the other B. See diagram below.

In English

3 In pairs, learner A tells a story to learner B in English.

4 Student B turns to the student on the left, another student A, and retells the story they have just heard, but this time in the native language. See diagram below.

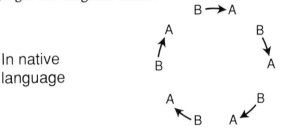

In native language

5 Student A retells the story in English to student B sitting on the left.

6 Allow the stories to come about halfway around the circle before you stop the story-telling.

7 Ask one student B to retell, in English, the last story they heard.

8 The student who originally told this story comments on how it has changed in the retelling.

9 Repeat stages 7 and 8 a number of times.

Stories move around the circle, told alternately in English and the native language. Student A will be telling the stories in English and listening to them in the native language. Student B will be telling the stories in the native language and listening to them in English. This is an intensive listening exercise where students have to spot differences.

REMARKS

1 This will only work in monolingual classes, preferably where the teacher knows the learners' native language.

2 A particular subject can be suggested for the stories, for example, at Christmas the topic could be 'A childhood Christmas memory'.

5.4 What is your text about?

LEVEL

Intermediate and above

TIME

40–60 minutes (depends on size of class)

LANGUAGE

Scanning, asking and answering questions

PROCEDURE

1 Each student writes a text of a given length in their native language about an interest or hobby, preferably something unusual or not well known to the group.

2 Redistribute the texts. The learners read them.

3 Learners pair off and work on one of the two texts.

4 Student A asks questions in English about the text student B has, and student B has to give short answers in English. Only information from the text can be used in the answers. Student B must not add any further information on the subject.

5 Questioning stops when student B decides that all the information in the text has been retrieved by student A.

6 Learners do the same for the second text.

7 You can pair off learners a few times, but make sure that the authors of the texts do not ask about their own texts.

REMARKS   This is a very good exercise in switching quickly from one language to another without becoming distracted.

5.5 How long will you manage?

LEVEL   **Lower-intermediate and upwards**

TIME   **Up to 30 minutes**

LANGUAGE   **Answering questions**

PROCEDURE   1 Learners get into pairs.

2 Student A asks student B questions in the native language such as: *How old are you? What size shoes do you take? What's your mother's name?* and student B answers them in English.

3 Student A can challenge the answer when it is grammatically incorrect.

4 This activity is a game and if student B mistakenly answers in the native language student A takes over answering questions and student B must ask them. When student A then answers in the wrong language the pair stops. The winning pair is the one that keeps going longest.

VARIATION 1   The whole class can ask one person questions and check the correctness of the answers. When the student makes a mistake, the person who asked the question takes his/her place.

VARIATION 2   The activity can also be done in writing but then the element of competition is lost. Once a certain number of questions have been answered, another pair takes the sheet of paper and checks the answers. You may choose some mistakes to discuss with the whole group.

VARIATION 3   The topic can be varied.

REMARKS

1 Each learner needs a partner who shares their native language.

2 This is a very good exercise for revealing interference mistakes: for example, in French you *have years* and not *are years old*, and in Polish you *wear* a certain size, not *take*.

5.6 Silent conversation

LEVEL

Lower-intermediate and above

TIME

30 minutes

LANGUAGE

Dialogue building

PROCEDURE

1 Students form pairs. Each pair has a single sheet of paper.

2 One student starts the activity by writing in the native language the equivalent of the English *How's life?*

3 The second student writes a reply either in the native language or in English, as they prefer, leaving space between the lines. The only rule is that students may write in English only those utterances they are absolutely sure are correct. If there is any doubt they should use the native language. This applies to words, phrases, or whole sentences.

4 The silent conversation develops freely, the students taking it in turns until the whole page has been filled.

5 Pairs exchange pieces of paper and read the conversations. They translate any parts of the conversation they are sure about. They write the translation above the native-language version.

6 The pieces of paper are circulated a few times until most of the conversation is in English.

7 Display the translations on a wall and discuss them with the whole class. Concentrate on the parts that have not been translated or have been translated incorrectly.

REMARKS

This activity works particularly well with less advanced students. They express themselves freely and are not limited by language problems. To make it more challenging for more advanced learners, it may be advisable to suggest a topic, such as 'Holes in the ozone layer'.

5.7 Home becomes England

LEVEL

Lower-intermediate and above

TIME

30–45 minutes

LANGUAGE

Language of signs and notices

PROCEDURE

1 Students close their eyes and try to recall five to eight signs or notices written in their native language that they see every day on their way from home to school, to the bus stop, when looking out of the window, and so on. The signs should contain words, not just place names. This part could be set for homework in the previous lesson.

2 Students write down the texts of the notices in their native language. Each one should be on a separate piece of paper.

3 Spread out all the notices, either on tables or on the floor. Students pick up whichever notice they know how to translate. They write the English translation on the reverse side and put the papers on a separate pile.

4 Meanwhile, draw a plan of a city, either on the board or on a very large piece of paper.

5 Students pick up a translated notice.

6 They draw on the plan a suitable place for the notice, for example: a park or a lawn for *Keep off the grass*, a building with shop windows for *Butcher*, a door for *Exit*.

7 The notices are attached to the plan with the English version displayed.

8 Students look at the completed plan and identify the places from the inscriptions. If in doubt they can always refer to the native-language version on the reverse.

VARIATION

If it is a large class, students can work in smaller groups, and in stage 8 they walk from city plan to city plan and identify the places.

REMARKS

1 One of the benefits of this activity is that students may acquire the habit of translating into English everything they see around them. Seeing the notices in the native language may also remind them of the translations done in class.

2 The activity clearly works only on courses held in a non-English-speaking country.

5.8 Chinese whispers

LEVEL

Lower-intermediate and above

TIME

30 minutes

LANGUAGE

General fluency practice, sentence structure

PROCEDURE

1 Seat the students in a big circle or in a way in which it is possible to pass sheets of paper around easily.

2 Each student takes a sheet of paper and writes at the top a sentence in their native language consisting of fifteen words.

3 Students pass the sheets to their left-hand neighbour.

4 Students translate the sentence they receive into English and write this below on the sheet. You can help with particular words, as required.

5 Students fold the papers in such a way that the native-language sentence is not visible and only the English translation can be seen.

6 They pass the sheets to the left again and translate the English sentence back into the native language.

7 As in stage 5, they fold the paper again so that only the sentence in the native language is visible and pass the sheet on to the left.

8 The translation procedure is repeated until there are five or six versions in each language.

9 Students pass on the sheets to the left once again and unfold the whole paper.

10 They get into pairs and look at the original sentence and the final English translation. Then they follow the stages of translation and decide if there are problems and differences between the original and the translations and why. Students read out those pairs of sentences they consider especially interesting.

11 Display all the translations and discuss mistakes and typical problems.

VARIATION 1

In stage 11 students read out the last translation. The author has to recognize his or her sentence.

VARIATION 2

With beginners, start with English sentences you know they can produce correctly. In order to do this let them browse through their notes and textbook. Make sure the chosen sentences are correct and from there continue the procedure from stage 5.

REMARKS

1 This activity offers insight into typical translation mistakes, such as problems with sentence structure, phrasing, and choice of vocabulary.

2 Students may ask the students who translated the sentence before them for clarification. This offers another opportunity for peer teaching.

5.9 Collective cultural consciousness

LEVEL

Advanced

TIME

60–75 minutes

LANGUAGE

Language of poetry

PROCEDURE

1 Explain to the learners that, even though they may claim that individually they do not 'know' any poetry, collectively they can probably reconstruct some poetry which is part of their shared cultural consciousness.

2 Individually learners try to recall parts of a poem or poems in their own language.

3 After a few minutes they circulate and recite, in their own language, the fragments they remember.

4 They should form groups of people who have thought of the same poem or of people who agree they want to work on a poem that one particular person has thought of.

5 Learners now work together reconstructing the poem in the original language. They write it down on a piece of paper. In the case of a long poem a fragment will be enough. The length will clearly depend on time available.

6 The papers are then passed to other groups who prepare a first translation into English.

7 The papers are now passed on to a third group who can make any changes they like to produce a more polished translation.

8 The final versions are read out to the whole class. The first group comments on whether the translation satisfies them, the second group comments on whether alterations to their version have improved the translation or not, and the class as a whole can suggest any other improvements.

VARIATION 1

If more than three groups are working, stage 7 can be extended so that other groups can see the poem and have a chance to make alterations.

VARIATION 2

It may be that the class as a whole decides on one particular poem. In this case they can still work in groups and then compare their different translations.

VARIATION 3

This activity also works with songs, or nursery rhymes remembered from childhood. The procedure is as above, but if there is a dance or game to accompany the song or nursery rhyme, students can 'perform' this while presenting the translation.

SAMPLE PRODUCT   This is a translation of a traditional Polish folk song, the words of which were written by a famous Polish poet, Franciszek Karpinski (1741–1825). The original title was 'Laura i Filon'.

Amanda and Ashley

The moon is down and all the dogs are sleeping,
Someone is clapping near the wood.
Surely my Ashley for me is waiting
And stay without him no more I could.

I have no time for setting my fair hair,
Cause I'm already two hours late.
Ashley by now must be in despair
Worrying what'll happen to our date.

REMARKS   1 This activity gives advanced learners the opportunity to use and discuss distinctions between near-synonyms which form a part of their passive vocabulary but which are rarely activated outside Cambridge Proficiency-style Reading Comprehension papers. For example, in the poem above the students spent some time discussing whether to use *clapping* or *applauding*.

2 See the Introduction to this chapter for possibilities of using this activity with multilingual classes.

5.10 Do you know this song?

LEVEL   Intermediate and above

TIME   30 minutes

LANGUAGE   Giving the gist, summarizing

PROCEDURE   1 Students form pairs and think of a song in their native language they know well. You can limit their choice by giving them a particular theme, such as Christmas carols, pop songs, or love songs.

2 Pairs do not reveal which song they have chosen. They write a five- to ten-sentence summary of the song in English.

3 In turns, one of each pair stands up and reads out the summary. The other pairs guess and write down the titles of the songs in the native language on a piece of paper.

4 The sheets are collected and pairs score a point for each correct answer.

VARIATION 1 Instead of stages 3 and 4, students can move around presenting their summaries to other pairs, who have to guess the titles.

VARIATION 2 This activity can also be done with poems or short stories.

REMARKS 1 This activity works best with monolingual groups of students.

2 It is important that the learners are not told about the competitive aspect of the activity before their write their summaries, otherwise they may deliberately make them unclear and difficult.

6 Games

Introduction

Games are frequently used in the language classroom to provide a light-hearted form of language practice, either with relatively free use of language, or where a particular structure is being repeated. In either case the emphasis is on playing the game and there is little room for correction during the activity.

In the games presented here, learners are involved not only in the playing, but also in the preparation of the games. It is in the preparation stage that the focus can be on form. This is the time for peer negotiation or consultation with the teacher. The learners thus have meaningful language practice before they play the game. This can be seen clearly, for example, where learners are writing instructions for others on how to play a game. The instructions must be clear and comprehensive and easy to follow, or the game will fail.

Learners still have the enjoyment of the game, as does the teacher, who can take part as a competitor, even in quizzes.

6.1 Mastermind

LEVEL	**All levels**
TIME	**About 60 minutes**, depending on the number in the group
LANGUAGE	**Asking questions**
PROCEDURE	**1** At the end of the preceding lesson tell the learners that they will be playing Mastermind in the next lesson. Explain that this is a quiz where each contestant has to answer questions on general knowledge and on a specialist topic. Tell them that they should now choose their special subject. This can be narrow, for example 'The Polish Mountain Rescue Service since 1945', or wide, for example 'Philosophy'. Given them a few minutes' thinking time.

2 Learners now dictate their subjects to the rest of the class. Dictate your own subject too.

3 At home everyone has to prepare one question for everyone else's subjects. They must also know the answer.

4 In the next lesson each person in turn comes to a chair in front of the group and everyone else takes it in turns to ask a question. A correct answer wins a point. In the case of an incorrect answer the questioner must supply the correct answer. The winner is the person with the most points.

VARIATION

Where the class is very big it may be necessary to split it into groups at the beginning of stage 2.

6.2 Presents

LEVEL

All levels

TIME

30–40 minutes

LANGUAGE

Describing people and objects, persuading

PROCEDURE

1 Learners take a blank sheet of paper from their exercise book and tear it up into four pieces.

2 On two pieces of paper they should write short descriptions of two objects, including the name of the object, for example: *a small brown leather shoulder bag*. Collect the pieces of paper.

3 On the other slips the learners write short descriptions of two people, for example: *a 62-year-old bachelor living alone who has a passion for cats and modern jazz*. These slips are collected in a different pile.

4 Shuffle the two piles separately.

5 Learners take two slips from the 'objects' pile and two from the 'people' pile.

6 Tell learners that the objects are presents and the descriptions are people they want to buy presents for.

7 Learners must now try to find suitable presents for the people whose descriptions they have. Working in pairs, student A, who might have the description of the 62-year-old bachelor, asks student B to suggest a present for this person. Student B tries to persuade student A that one of his/her two objects would make a suitable present. Student A can then decide to 'buy' the object or not. Student A then asks about a present for the second person.

8 Then students reverse roles and B asks A to suggest possible presents.

9 Learners move on to work with other partners.

10 As the 'buyers' find suitable presents they write them down on the slip of paper describing that person. It is permissible to buy a lot of presents for each person. The 'sellers' can sell their objects as many times as possible and they should keep a record of how many times they sell them.

11 As a final stage the whole class decides who are the easiest people to buy presents for. In other words, which people 'received' the most objects, and which are the best presents (those objects most frequently 'sold').

VARIATIONS

The variations here depend on how learners are instructed to write the descriptions of objects and people. They may be asked, for example, to write a noun phrase with two or more adjectives, or a noun phrase plus relative clause, or to write a full paragraph describing a person. The fuller the description, the more time is spent on the 'negotiation' stage. It may be easier for learners to describe someone if they have a specific person (relative or friend) in mind.

6.3 Drawing prepositions

LEVEL

Lower-intermediate

TIME

20–30 minutes

LANGUAGE

Spatial prepositions, giving instructions

PROCEDURE

1 Explain that the learners are going to prepare an obstacle race, which will be drawn on the board. Invite a student to do the drawing or be prepared to do it yourself.

2 Learners suggest obstacles and their locations, for example: *Let's put a big hole in the top left hand corner. What about a river below that? O.K. Now put a wall between the river and the hole.* The suggestions are drawn on the board.

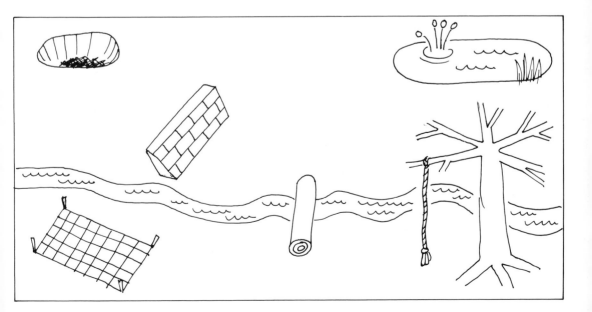

3 Divide the class into teams. Each team copies down the course on a separate piece of paper and decides on a route around it. They draw the route on the paper.

4 Circulate the route maps clockwise to the next group.

5 On a separate piece of paper groups now write a description of the route they have just received, but should include three prepositional 'mistakes'. For example, the map shows a route *around the pond* but the description says *through the pond*.

6 Pass the route maps and their accompanying descriptions to the next groups, still moving in a clockwise direction.

7 Explain that each group now has a route map and a description which contains three mistakes. At a given signal from you they will have to read the paragraph, compare it with the map, and find the mistakes.

8 The first group to identify the mistakes correctly is the winner.

VARIATION

In pairs or small groups, students draw an obstacle course on a single sheet of paper with a given number of obstacles of their own choosing. They also mark the route on the course. They pass their routes to another group/pair in a clockwise direction. At a given signal from you, the groups start to write, on a separate piece of paper, a description of how to get round the course according to the route they have just received. The first group to finish writing, and thus to 'complete' the course, is the winner. There should be a checking stage in which routes and their accompanying descriptions are returned to the group which drew the route. These groups decide if the route they drew has been accurately described. Any doubts may lead to a 'Steward's Inquiry'—you have to decide who is right.

6.4 Irregular verbs match

LEVEL

Lower-intermediate

TIME

10 minutes

LANGUAGE

Irregular verbs

PROCEDURE

1 Learners stand up and form pairs.

2 Student A gives the infinitive form of a verb and student B has to supply the simple past form.

3 If they agree that the answer is right, B has the chance to test A in the same way. They continue, alternating turns, until one person either does not know the answer or, according to the questioner, makes a mistake. Any disputes should be referred to you as umpire.

4 The student who does not know, or who has made a mistake, sits down and the remaining student looks for another partner.

5 The game continues until only one person remains standing. In the case of a deadlock with two or three people remaining, it can go to a tie-break with you giving an infinitive and the first person to answer winning.

VARIATION 1   In stage 5, if learners have a list of irregular verbs available, the learners who are sitting can refer to this to test the remaining contenders further in the same way.

VARIATION 2   Other tenses and constructions can of course be used instead.

6.5 Effective shopping

LEVEL   **Lower-intermediate**

TIME   **30–40 minutes**

LANGUAGE   **Language of shopping, describing objects**

PROCEDURE   1 Divide learners into two groups, shoppers and shopkeepers.

2 The shoppers prepare a ten-item shopping list to give to another person. As someone else will have to do the shopping, the list should be as detailed as possible, for example not just *a fuse*, but *a ten-amp fuse for a blender*. It may help the preparation if the learners simply remember ten items they have bought recently.

3 The shopkeepers as a group decide who is to run what kind of shop. The activity probably works best if there is no overlap and everyone runs a different kind of shop. Individually they decide on ten different items they have in stock and what quantities they have of each item. They should also write detailed descriptions of their stock.

4 The shoppers swap lists and the shopkeepers move to different parts of the room.

5 Announce that the shops are open for a limited period of time and tell the learners that there will be a competition to find the most successful shopper and shopkeeper. Shopkeepers say what kind of shops they run. They could make a label to remind the shoppers.

6 The shoppers move from shop to shop, 'buying' items on their lists.

7 As the shopkeepers 'sell' their goods they should adjust the quantities left in stock and keep a note of the number of sales they make. NB: selling three fuses to one customer would count as one sale, selling one fuse each to three different customers would count as three sales.

8 The shopkeepers can try to persuade their customers to buy other goods if they do not have the required ones in stock.

9 The most successful shopper is the one who has found most items on their list. The most successful shopkeeper is the one who has had the greatest number of sales.

VARIATION

This activity also works if learners write a shopping list for themselves of ten items they actually need or would like to buy and in this case they do not swap the lists as in stage 4. There is then no need to write a detailed description of the item as the details will emerge as they go around the shops.

6.6 Travel quiz

LEVEL

Elementary

TIME

20–30 minutes

LANGUAGE

Simple present, times, prices

PROCEDURE

1 Give learners a limited time to write down any exact travel information they actually know—exact times, dates of departure, fares, routes, conditions of travel. The information must be real and they must be sure that it is correct. You may need to restrict this to a local area, or the town where the students are studying.

2 Form the class into two teams, or, if it is a large class, into an even number of teams.

3 Within the teams, learners pool the information they have noted down, explaining what the times and fares and so on refer to. As a group they decide on ten questions they are going to ask another team, for example: *Does the morning express to Warsaw stop at Malbork? How much does it cost to fly to London and back? How often does the ferry go to Helsinki?*

4 Bring the two teams together, or, if there are more than two, pair off groups.

5 The first team asks a question and the second has a few moments to consult before giving their answer. If they are right they get a point.

6 The second team asks their first question and so the game proceeds, teams alternating questions.

6.7 The 'why' game

LEVEL   Lower-intermediate and above

TIME   20–30 minutes

LANGUAGE   Asking questions

PROCEDURE   1 Students write down a set number of *why* questions (five or ten). The questions can be of a personal, professional, or general nature.
Examples:
Why are there no women in this group?
Why is the sky blue?
Why is the exchange rate of the dollar going down?
They should be questions where the student genuinely wants an answer or opinion.

2 Students stand up and move around the room, working with different partners in turn. In pairs they ask each other a question that they have written down. Students get a point if they give an answer that satisfies or convinces the questioner. When a question is answered satisfactorily, it is crossed off the list.

3 Learners now change partners and repeat the procedure, either with a new question (if their previous one was satisfactorily answered) or repeating the same question.

4 The game continues until all questions have been answered or until a set time has passed. Unanswered questions can now be opened up to the whole group for discussion.

5 The winner is the person who has answered most questions satisfactorily.

6.8 The chat show

LEVEL   All levels

TIME   20–40 minutes

LANGUAGE   Asking questions, especially in the simple past

PROCEDURE   1 Explain, if necessary, that a chat show is a radio or television programme where a presenter talks to well-known guests who also chat among themselves as the programme develops.

2 The learners each choose a well-known person, either living or dead, and write this name down in their exercise books. It should be a person whose biographical details they are familiar with. They should not show the name to other people in the class.

3 Explain that the learners are to appear on the chat show as these people, and that the programme will last a fixed time, for example fifteen minutes. Their task is to guess the identity of their fellow guests.

4 Begin the show by addressing questions yourself to all the guests as a group.
Examples:
When did you first become interested in politics?
What was the first film you made?
Why did you commit suicide?
What do you regard as the greatest achievement in your life?
If a question is relevant to more than one guest, those people should all answer it in turn.

5 As the programme goes on, each 'guest' can address questions to the others. They should not, however, address questions to specific guests but to all the others as a group.

6 When the time is up, learners write down who they think the other guests are.

7 Ask all the guests to reveal their identities. Learners score one point for each successful guess. The winner is the person with the most correct guesses.

VARIATION 1	If learners are familiar with the format of chat shows, an additional stage can be introduced at the beginning. They should each write down on a slip of paper two or three typical chat show questions. Collect these and incorporate them into your questioning.
VARIATION 2	Alternatively you can nominate a student as presenter and become a guest yourself, or allow all the guests to ask questions from the start.

6.9 Tennis

LEVEL	**Lower-intermediate and above**
TIME	**10–15 minutes**
LANGUAGE	**'We all', 'All of us', 'None of us'**
PROCEDURE	**1** Learners work in pairs with one sheet of paper between them.
	2 They toss a coin to see who starts.
	3 The first person 'serves' by writing a sentence which is true for everyone in the room, including the teacher.

Examples:
We all speak English.
All of us are right-handed.
None of us are mountaineers.

4 The second person can either accept the 'serve' and return it by writing a second sentence, or 'call a fault'. A fault occurs when the information is not correct or as required, for example, *Paul is a mountaineer*, or when there is a grammatical mistake. If a 'serve' or a 'return' is faulty, the player does not score and the 'ball' returns to the opponent.

5 The game continues, scoring as for tennis, until one person wins or until you call 'tie-break'. In the event of a tie-break each player writes one more sentence without comment. They read their sentences out and you, or the group as a whole, decide who wins. The criterion can be grammatical or factual accuracy, or any other.

VARIATION 1

This game format may be used for other grammatical structures, such as present perfect, but with factual content still important and checkable. In this way it is more of a game and less of a drill.

VARIATION 2

Instead of the factual content having to be true for all of the group, you may stipulate that it should be true only for both players, for example, *We both like football.*

REMARKS

If players have disputes over factual information or grammatical accuracy, you are the umpire.

6.10 Invent a game

LEVEL

All levels

TIME

30–40 minutes

LANGUAGE

Giving instructions

PROCEDURE

1 Divide the class into an even number of small groups of four to five people.

2 Each group has to invent a game which can be played by four to five players using only what materials happen to be available in the classroom or in the immediate vicinity.

3 As a group they write down the rules for playing the game on a separate piece of paper.

4 Pair off the groups.

5 The paired groups exchange rules.

6 Groups read the rules they have been given and in turn play the game with the second team as a silent audience. They are not allowed to ask the authors for clarification before they start, and the members of the second team (the authors) are not allowed to comment during the demonstration of the game.

7 When a group has demonstrated how they think the game should be played, the authors are allowed to comment.

VARIATION 1

You can be more directive by giving the game a name. For example, once, after a friendly dispute between colleagues over the exact meaning of the phrase 'ducks and drakes', we asked our students to devise a game with that title. Not surprisingly all of the groups came up with team games which were quite different.

VARIATION 2

If you can hold your class in an adventure playground, fitness trail, or somewhere with swings, roundabouts, and slides, you can play 'obstacle races'. In groups the learners prepare a route around all the obstacles, with tasks to be performed at each. They write down details of the route and exchange these with another group. Then everyone has to complete the circuit in accordance with the instructions they have received. To make it really competitive you can time each team as they complete the circuit according to the instructions they received, and according to their own instructions. The fastest team for each set of instructions wins.

REMARKS

The focus here is on playing games but it also gives learners meaningful practice in writing clear and precise instructions. They can see from what the other group does how well they have carried out the writing part of this activity. This is why at stage 6 groups are not allowed to ask for clarification or to comment. Everything depends on how effectively the instructions are written.

7 Exam preparation

Introduction

These activities were produced for students preparing for the Cambridge First Certificate examination, but they can also be used with students preparing for other examinations which feature the same test types, for example cloze or multiple choice. They can also be used with non-examination classes.

They offer learners practice in dealing with examination-type exercises without doing old papers. By being involved in the production of the exercises before carrying them out, students are taken 'behind the scenes' and given an insight into how the exercises are constructed and what they are required to do for each type of test. They can be given this practice without even being aware that it represents examination preparation, so that pre-exam tension is lessened.

In some activities, for example 'Listening comprehension' (7.7) or 'We test you, you test us' (7.5), it is necessary for the learners to have had previous experience with exam-style tasks. In this case they are encouraged to consider the kind of tasks that are normally encountered in the exam and the different kinds of trap that await them. Here too, learners draw on the knowledge they already have. Again the aim is to sensitize them to the rationale behind the tests, to familiarize them with the mechanism of the tasks, and so to improve their performance.

The product of some of these activities is exam practice material which can be used by other groups of learners, either in class or for self-study, for example 7.2, 7.5.

7.1 Ideal classroom

LEVEL	**Lower-intermediate and above**
TIME	**30 minutes**
LANGUAGE	**Planning and talking about a picture, speculating, giving reasons**
PROCEDURE	**1** Learners work in pairs, first designing and then drawing what they consider to be an ideal classroom. They should, however, not label it in any way; for example, they should not write what the equipment is called or what its function is.

2 Two pairs exchange drawings. They look at each others' drawings and try to work out why this is an ideal classroom and what the purpose of the particular items is.

3 When they have discussed the drawings, the pairs who exchanged drawings swap partners.

4 Each new pair should have one drawing. The person who interpreted this drawing, not the original designer, comments on the design. The designer listens and then confirms, or amends, what the other student has said.

5 The twinned pairs then exchange drawings and repeat stage 4.

6 Display all the designs. Learners can then choose the classroom they would most like to work in.

SAMPLE PRODUCT

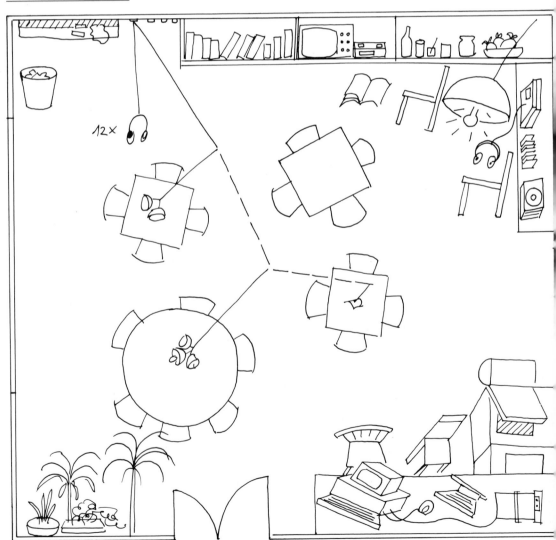

VARIATION

In stage 4, the learners who interpret their colleagues' drawings may 'colour' them by saying what colour scheme there is in the classroom in general, and what colours the particular elements are. This adds a new, revealing dimension to the interpretation stage.

REMARKS

1 This activity is a good preparation for the oral elements of exams which involve talking about a picture.

2 Learners learn to talk about a picture in different ways. They start by planning one, and then interpret another, knowing only that it is supposed to be an ideal classroom.

3 This activity says a lot about the learners' feelings towards the classroom environment, and it may give you some ideas on how to organize the classroom to make them feel more comfortable in it. It is interesting to observe that in many cases, ideal classrooms have flowers, lots of space and colour, often no rows of chairs but circles or semicircles, and plenty of bookshelves.

7.2 Our dialogue

LEVEL

All levels

TIME

60 minutes

LANGUAGE

Open dialogue, predicting, appropriacy, reference

PROCEDURE

1 In pairs, learners find an area of interest they have in common. Do not interrupt but allow conversations to develop (in English).

2 After ten minutes stop the conversations and ask learners individually to reflect on the development of the conversation, what was said, in what order, and by whom.

3 Still in the same pairs, learners recall a fragment of their conversation in as much detail as they can.

4 Give each pair a blank piece of paper, for example A5 (it is essential that throughout the activity all the students are writing on pieces of paper of the same size).

5 Give them instructions on how to write out the conversation. They should write on one side of the paper only, and should draw a margin on the left. In the margin they will write only the initials of the speakers. Between each utterance they should leave a space.

6 Give them a time limit, for example ten minutes, to write as much as they can. The final product should look like this:

A	Have you got a car?
B	No, I haven't. Why?
A	You've got one problem less. There are so many thieves in the Gdansk area. Every other week I wake up and find my car has been broken into.
B	Maybe you should buy a car alarm.
A	Yes, I agree, but I think my husband should do that. He drives more often.
B	Yes, I see, but as I haven't got a car I've got a lot of problems too, controlling my expenses. For example, I often have to take a taxi, which is expensive these days.

Make sure there are no mistakes in the texts.

7 When the texts are ready, learners draw horizontal lines to separate each utterance and then cut along these lines, leaving the left margin untouched. The sheet takes the form of a collection of slips of paper with utterances held together by the left margin, which contains the names of the speakers.

8 Learners then choose which slips are to be concealed from the reader by folding them back. They should not conceal two consecutive utterances.

9 Give each pair a second blank sheet of the same size as in stage 5. They put the blank sheet under the fragmented conversation and fasten the two pieces of paper with a paper clip.

10 Collect all the papers and redistribute them.

11 The pairs now try to fill in the spaces in the dialogue they have just received. They have to take into consideration not only the grammar, logic, and style, but also the size of the gap to be filled in. They write on the sheet slipped underneath the fragmented conversation.

A	Have you got a car?
B	No, I haven't
A	You've got one problem less. There are so many thieves in the Gdansk area. Every other week I wake up and find my car has been broken into.
B	A car alarm would scare them away. You could buy one.
A	Yes, I agree, but I think my husband should do that. He drives more often.
B	Every wife would love her husband if he bought a car alarm.

12 The activity ends with a display of the original conversation next to the new versions and a group discussion of the alternatives.

VARIATION 1

At the beginning of the activity you can specify a topic, for example a film seen by both the learners, the weather, or a mutual friend.

VARIATION 2

Stage 11 can be repeated so that students work on more than one dialogue. In this case collect all the papers. Detach the second sheets and redistribute the fragmented conversations with a new blank piece of paper.

VARIATION 3

After stage 11 display the complete original conversations, and redistribute the second sheets of paper to pairs. Each pair tries to match this sheet with the original.

REMARKS

1 If you are concerned that learners might not cut up the conversation in the right way, or if you would rather decide which parts of the conversation should be concealed, then collect the texts from the learners and carry out the technical tasks described in stages 7 and 8 yourself. This is, however, quite time-consuming, and it may slow down the flow of the lesson.

2 If a photocopier is available, the fragmented conversations that are prepared in stage 7 can be photocopied so that they are more manageable. In this way learners would have their own copies to write on in class or at home.

3 The activity corresponds to exam questions involving completing a dialogue. See, for example, FCE—Use of English, Part A.

7.3 What's in the picture?

LEVEL
All levels

TIME
30–45 minutes

LANGUAGE
Talking about a picture, spatial arrangement

PROCEDURE
1 Tell the learners that the board is a canvas where a picture is to be painted. Draw a grid on the 'canvas' (see below).

2 Learners copy the grid into their exercise books, and in pairs label the segments by writing in the words describing location, for example, *at the top, in the top left-hand corner*, like this:

		at the top	
on the left			
in the bottom left-hand corner			

3 When all the pairs are ready, discuss the labels given to the spaces and any possible variations.

4 Learners individually draw their own pictures, filling all the spaces.

5 The exercise now becomes a paired listen-and-draw activity, where student A describes the picture and student B draws it. They then reverse roles.

6 Finally, in pairs learners compare the original picture and the picture drawn from instructions. You can organize an exhibition.

SAMPLE PRODUCT

VARIATION

In stage 4 you can suggest a topic for the picture, one that perhaps relates to a topic area discussed in class, or to the time of year. In this way you can check previous language input. For example, if disasters have recently been discussed, learners may be invited to draw a scene after a flood or an earthquake. It is also possible to introduce a new topic.

REMARKS

1 This activity is a variation on the listen-and-draw technique which is very productive, as it pre-teaches the language concerning the organization of a picture, and at the same time offers an opportunity to revise vocabulary or introduce new language.

2 You should make it clear that in stage 4, learners draw one picture whose elements fill all the spaces, and not sixteen separate pictures, one in each segment.

7.4 What do you mean?

LEVEL

Intermediate and above

TIME

45 minutes

LANGUAGE

Structural reformulations

PROCEDURE

1 Each learner thinks about a grammar problem or structure. Give various suggestions, such as reported speech, comparatives, active and passive, either by naming the problem or by giving examples.

2 Everyone writes a sentence using their chosen structure. As learners write their sentences, make sure they are correct.

3 Still working individually, learners paraphrase their own sentences so that the new sentence has the same meaning but uses different structures. Check that the transformations are correct in terms of both meaning and grammar.

4 Learners now dictate their second sentences to the rest of the class followed by the beginnings of the first sentences. Make sure that the latter are as short as possible, just enough to suggest the structure which is to be elicited. The rest of the class write them down.

5 When all the sentences have been dictated, learners reconstruct the original sentences individually or in pairs. This stage can also be done as homework.

6 Finally, the sentences reconstructed by the learners are read out and discussed. Their original authors act as 'experts'.

SAMPLE PRODUCT

Student's problem: mixed conditional

With help from the teacher: *If I had worn a coat yesterday I wouldn't be ill today.*
New sentence: *It's a pity I didn't wear a coat yesterday because I am ill today.*
Dictation: *It's a pity I didn't wear a coat yesterday because I am ill today. If . . .*

VARIATION

To make the task more difficult, after learners have written their first sentences redistribute the slips of paper and ask another student to paraphrase the sentence. Then this student dictates the new sentence and the beginning of the old one to the whole class. An additional element of surprise is to see whether the original authors can reconstruct their own sentences.

REMARKS

1 This activity makes learners aware of the mechanism of structural reformulations. It helps them to realize that it is not only a technical exercise, but a question of meaning as well.

They get double practice by not only writing a sentence and paraphrasing it, but also paraphrasing other learners' sentences.

2 If the class is big, divide learners into subgroups. Ten is the maximum number of sentences to be dictated, written down, and transformed.

7.5 We test you, you test us

LEVEL

Lower-intermediate and above

TIME

90 minutes

LANGUAGE

Writing tests

PROCEDURE

1 Elicit from learners all the various testing techniques they have ever encountered in their learning experience. Ask them either to name the test, for example cloze test or multiple choice, or describe it, for example: *It is a test where you listen to the tape; It is an exercise where you choose one word out of four given to complete a sentence.*

2 Write down the suggested test techniques using their formal names.

3 Divide learners into groups of three, and ask them to browse through their exercise books for items and problems which could be tested.

4 Each group prepares a test for another group comprising twenty-five test items. The format and layout is up to each group. Each test may use different test techniques but the instructions must be clear.

5 As learners write their tests, check for correctness.

6 When the groups have written their tests, they should produce a key on a separate sheet of paper.

7 Give each test and key a matching number.

8 The tests are circulated and other groups do them.

9 Make keys available by request when a group has finished.

10 Finally, discuss the 'troublemakers'—the items that gave problems to most learners.

VARIATION 1

After stage 2, you can run a poll or discussion in small groups on who prefers which test and why, or which tests are most disliked. This gives the learners a chance to practise the formal terminology, which will come in handy later in the course of the exercise.

VARIATION 2 For stage 8, you can collect the tests, photocopy them, and give them out as homework. Then the correction and discussion stage opens the next lesson.

VARIATION 3 You can limit the subject-matter of the tests, for example to vocabulary or grammar.

SAMPLE PRODUCT

I. Fill in the blanks with the missing prepositions:

1. Jane was just going out of the shop when she bumped ... her mother.

2. Everything was alright when he was working by himself, but when he started working with Charlie he ran ... difficulties.

II. Choose the correct alternative:

1. We were walking down the street when we ... Peter.

   a. met   c. were meeting.
   b. have met   d. will meet.

2. They ... their mother since last Christmas.

   a. didn't see   c. weren't seeing
   b. haven't seen d. will not see.

III. Complete the words correctly:

1. Who was the most famous play... in the 16th century?

   a. -writer
   b. -write
   c. -wright
   d. -righter

2. He left me alone, it was (...) loyal (...) of him

   a. il-
   b. dis-
   c. -less
   d. un-

REMARKS **1** A necessary pre-condition for this activity is that learners have come across various exam papers before.

2 This is a very good revision exercise because learners have to browse through their exercise books for test items and then select some for use in the test.

3 The teacher is relieved of the task of writing and marking tests outside the classroom. Learners do it themselves and the role of the teacher in the lesson is to make sure that the tests they prepare are correct.

4 Learners also get practice in writing instructions and in so doing become more aware of the importance of reading instructions carefully.

7.6 Letters

LEVEL — **Intermediate and above**

TIME — **45 minutes**

LANGUAGE — **Grammar revision**

PROCEDURE —

1 Learners think of a letter they should have written a long time ago. Stress that it does not matter whether the letter is in their native language, in English, or in any other language, or whether it is of a private or business nature. Suggest a suitable length for the letter.

2 Students write the letter in English. As they write make sure the letters are correct.

3 Each letter is then passed to another student, who condenses the letter, and writes it down in skeleton form on a separate sheet of paper. Explain which types of words they should remove. Give them an example sentence on the board, for example:

Original sentence
Thank you very much for your last letter and I am very sorry I have not replied for such a long time.

After transformation
Thank/ very much/ last letter/ and/ I/ be/ sorry/ not reply/ such a long time/.

Explain that verbs must in the infinitive form, and if they were originally in the negative, the infinitives must be preceded by 'not'. All pronouns must be given in this form: *I, you, he, she,* and so on, and not as *me, your, him.* The word order must be maintained.

4 As they write the skeleton, check that they are doing it properly.

5 Next the learners put the skeleton version of the letter on top of the original, fasten them together with a paper clip, and pass the sheets to another student.

6 Learners now reconstruct in writing the original letter on the basis of the skeleton, not looking at the bottom sheet. They should write on a separate piece of paper.

7 When they have finished they can check their version with the original, which serves as a key.

8 Encourage the learners to consult you when they are in doubt, as there may be more than one possibility.

9 The procedure of passing on the skeleton letters for reconstruction is repeated several times.

SAMPLE PRODUCT

Dear Joanna,

I don't know how to apologize for not writing to you for so long. I really wanted to send you my best New Year wishes but, I know it is hard to believe, I couldn't get postage stamps! It was really impossible! And I hoped you would come to Poland for Christmas and stay with us for even a couple of days.

Do believe me that for the last three months there has not been a day when I haven't thought about you. I am so curious about what you are doing now.

I am looking forward to hearing from you soon,

Yours,

Skeleton letter:
1 I/ not know/ how/ apologize/ you/ not write/ you/ so long/.
2 I/ really/ want/ send you/ best New Year wishes/ but/ I know/ hard/ believe/ I/ cannot/ get/ postage stamps.
3 It/ be/ really impossible.
4 And/ I hope/ you come/ Poland/ Christmas/ and/ stay/ we/ even/ couple of days/.
5 Do/ believe/ I/ the last three months/ there/ be not/ a day/ when/ I/ not think/ you.
6 I/ be curious/ what you/ do/ now/.
7 I/ look forward/ hear/ you/ soon.

VARIATION

The same technique can be applied to writing stories, jokes, notes, and memos. The procedure, however, remains the same.

7.7 Listening comprehension

LEVEL

Lower-intermediate and above

TIME

90 minutes

LANGUAGE

Writing questions and listening comprehension texts

PROCEDURE

1 Learners recall what types of listening comprehension questions they have encountered in their learning experience, and what the typical problems and traps were.

2 Learners form groups of three or four. They choose one or two test types, for example multiple choice, completing a grid, ticking boxes, labelling diagrams.

3 In their groups students make up a text which could be used for a listening comprehension test. They do not write this, they only discuss it in outline. It could be an interview, a person giving instructions on how to do something, or someone telling a story.

4 They then prepare a question paper to go with this text. They should include the kind of misleading items they often encounter in such tests, but they should not write the answers. Every student in the group writes out the questions on a separate piece of paper so that there are multiple copies.

5 Check the question papers for clarity and correctness.

6 All the sets of question papers are collected and redistributed to other groups.

7 Groups read the question papers they have just received. They have to prepare a text for listening comprehension on the basis of this question paper. They decide on what form the text should take, for example a dialogue or an announcement. They decide which answers are 'correct'.

8 They make up their own text which contains the answers to all the questions. For example, a multiple choice question could be:

Mr Smith . . .
a. has three children
b. has two sons
c. has one daughter
d. lives with his children

Students choose an answer, for example *has three children*, and then incorporate the information into the text. The answer does not have to be explicit and the information can be spread throughout the text. An example of a text could be:

'Mr Smith lives with his daughter in Manchester. She is not married but has a young son. Her twin brother, Mark, lives in Australia, and they have not seen him since the wedding of Julia, Mr Smith's favourite daughter.'

9 As a group they write out the listening comprehension text.

10 Make sure that the texts produced by the students are correct and that the questions can be answered from them.

11 The groups decide how to present the text. They practise the presentation quietly so that other groups do not overhear.

12 One group gives out their set of question papers to all the other groups. Make sure that all the students can see the question paper.

13 The group then presents their text and the other groups listen and discuss the answers within their group. The group presenting the test checks the answers.

14 Repeat stages 12 and 13 so that every group presents their text to the other groups.

VARIATION   In stage 11, if cassette or tape recorders are available, groups can record their texts. The material can be used with other classes.

SAMPLE PRODUCT

Question paper

1 Two men were travelling by:

a. plane

b. car

c. train

d. on foot

2 The obstacle they encountered was:

a. a road accident

b. a terrorist attack

c. an explosion in a nuclear power station

d. a person with a heart attack

3 What did the victim look like?

a. strawberry jam

b. ketchup

c. a white sheet

d. not mentioned

4 What did they decide to do with the victim?

a. take him to a coroner

b. wash him

c. ignore him

d. rob him

5 Where does this piece of information come from?

a. TV

b. a radio broadcast

c. a newspaper

d. gossip

6 Both the witnesses looked:

a. not well

b. fairly well

c. quite well

d. rather well

Text

(Sounds of a train)

Mary: John, have you heard what happened to Peter on his last assignment?

John: Oh, Peter from the BBC who always travels by British Airways. He looked fairly well the last time I met him.

Mary: Yes, exactly, that one. He and his friend were travelling down the road, in a desert. The temperature was so high that the road was nearly melting. They stopped for a while in an oasis to rest a bit and get some water. By the way, would you like to have a sandwich?

John: Yes please. Have you got any ketchup?

Mary: No, John, but I have some strawberry jam. To continue. The oasis was attacked by a rebel group. After the explosion one person was thrown onto the melting road by the blast. You can imagine what he looked like. Both went as white as sheets. They ran back quickly to the car and drove away. They were really frightened.

John: Oh, what a terrible story. Have you any more sandwiches?

Key 1.b 2.b 3.d 4.c 5.d 6.a

REMARKS

1 In this activity students work backwards. They begin by discussing types of listening comprehension questions, prepare the questions and texts themselves, and then do the test. In this way the learners get a better understanding of the mechanism of listening comprehension tests.

2 Learners usually get very involved and a lot of dramatic preparation goes on in the presentation stage. They produce various background noises: in the case of a telephone conversation they try to make the voice sound as if the person is really speaking on the phone, for example. They should therefore be given extra time for practice before the presentation stage.

7.8 Cloze test

LEVEL

Lower-intermediate and above

TIME

60–90 minutes

LANGUAGE

Grammar revision

PROCEDURE

1 Individually, students look through their exercise books and recently corrected work and select six or seven words or phrases that they have learnt recently. They also pick out one or two grammar items they have had problems with, for example *such a, used to doing, suggested going*.

2 Students get into groups of three or four. In their groups they discuss their word lists and select up to twenty lexical items.

3 Students plan a text around these items.

4 As a group they write the text, incorporating some, or all, of the grammar items they listed in stage 1.

5 Check that the completed texts are correct.

6 Students rewrite the texts leaving blank spaces. They can omit either words from their lexical lists or elements of the grammatical items.

7 Make sure that only one word is missing from each space and that the blanks are numbered.

8 The groups prepare the keys to accompany their tests.

9 The tests circulate and each group has to do each test and then check with the key. Make sure students do not write in the blanks provided, but on separate sheets of paper.

10 Hold a brief discussion about which items caused the greatest problems.

<table>
<tr><td>VARIATION 1</td><td>After stage 5 students exchange texts, and other groups remove the words and prepare the key. This may mean that the items listed by the original group are not tested. However, it does mean that even the authors can work on their own text.</td></tr>
</table>

VARIATION 1

After stage 5 students exchange texts, and other groups remove the words and prepare the key. This may mean that the items listed by the original group are not tested. However, it does mean that even the authors can work on their own text.

VARIATION 2

Give the learners a list of items to be tested. They write a text around them and then the items are removed. In this case you have control over the items and, as the texts circulate, the same items are tested many times in different contexts.

VARIATION 3

To make the exercise easier, students removing words can prepare a list of those words, but in a jumbled-up order. Then in stage 9 students doing the test have to put the words in the right places.

VARIATION 4

Instead of rewriting texts in stage 6, students can take scissors and cut the word out, but in such a way that the fragment containing the word is not completely removed, but folded underneath the page. In this way instant reference and key are provided.

7.9 Contextualizing the question

LEVEL

Intermediate and above

TIME

40–50 minutes

LANGUAGE

Speed reading, intensive reading

PROCEDURE

1 Each student writes three comprehension-style questions on separate slips of paper. The only restriction is that questions should refer to a third person, that is they should not include *you*, *I*, or *we*. Students may need examples of what is required before being able to produce suitable questions.

2 Collect the slips and put them into a hat or a paper bag. Before the students put their questions in, make sure the questions are grammatically correct.

3 Shake the bag well so that the slips are mixed up.

4 Students get into pairs and take three slips at random from the bag.

5 Each pair writes a short paragraph which contains the answers to the three questions. The answers do not have to be explicit, they may be implied.

6 Display all the texts on the wall.

7 Collect all the questions the pairs selected and put them back in the bag with the remaining ones. Shake the bag so that the slips are well mixed.

8 Students come to the front of the class and each person takes one question from the bag. Individually they try to find an answer in the texts on the wall. If they find an answer they stick the question under the text, and take another question from the bag. If they cannot find an answer they put the question in a specially designated place, for example on your desk, and take another one from the bag.

9 They carry on until there are no questions left in the bag.

10 The students now go back to the texts, read each one in turn, and check that the questions do go with the text. They can put a mark on a question if they think it does not go with the text.

11 Discuss any doubts that arise with the whole class. The original authors can also reveal which questions led to the creation of their texts.

SAMPLE PRODUCT   Questions produced in stage 1:

```
Is she angry?                        What is love?
What is on TV tonight?               How long do bears sleep in winter?
What colour did they mention?        What is his favourite colour?
How far is it from Warsaw to         What made him laugh?
  Gdansk?                            What was her name?
How can you earn money without
  working?
```

The following three questions led to the production of the texts below:

```
Is she angry?
How far is it from Warsaw to Gdansk?
What is his favourite colour?


After winning the pools, a happy young couple decided to buy a car. But
what make and where to buy it? They were living in Gdansk but they decided
to go over 300 kilometres to the capital of Poland. After a long
discussion they agreed to buy a Mercedes. A problem arose when they had to
choose the colour. She wanted white but he preferred red. And there were
no cars in two colours to please them both. So he did as he pleased. On
the way back from Warsaw she did not speak to him.
```

Additional questions matched by the students:

```
What does he like?
What colour did they mention?
How can you earn money without working?
```

REMARKS

1 This activity gives practice in speed reading and intensive reading, but it also encourages learners to think of the possible traps contained in reading comprehension questions.

2 At the end of stage 7, it is possible that there will be more or fewer than three questions under each text. It may happen that there are some questions which can be answered from more than one text, for example, the question *What is his name?* could apply to any text where there is a man's name. It is also possible that some distractor questions can, completely by accident, be answered from a particular text.

7.10 Word building

LEVEL

Intermediate and above

TIME

60 minutes

LANGUAGE

Families of words, grammatical categories

PROCEDURE

1 In groups of three or four, students try to think of a large family of words deriving from a particular headword. To make their task easier give them an example, such as *courage: courageous, encourage, discourage*, or *decision: decisive, decide, indecisive, decisively*, and so on.

2 When they are ready, give each group a number of small pieces of paper, or cards, all the same size. They write on each piece one word from the family of words. On the reverse they write the grammatical category of the word: noun, abstract noun, verb, etc. If they have more than one word in each category, they must add short definitions or synonyms beside the category for those words.

3 Distribute dictionaries. Students check the existence and spelling of *all* the words, and their grammatical categories.

4 Looking through the dictionaries, students will come across words they had not thought of. They can write these, with their grammatical categories, on other pieces of paper.

5 Students put aside their cards for the time being. Elicit from them what negative prefixes they know, for example *mis-, dis-, in-, un-*.

6 Students now form negatives of words in their families, checking them in dictionaries and adding the words with their categories to their piles. They should also make a note that the word is negative, by writing 'neg.' or putting a minus sign.

7 Students arrange all the words in a pile in such a way that the categories are face up. Only the top card with the root word is displayed with the word facing up.

8 Before they pass on their sets of words, students should look at the category side of their own words and try to remember what word is on the other side.

9 Then groups exchange piles.

10 They first identify the family by looking at the top card. Then they look at the category on the next card and try to think of the words that is on the other side. They turn over the card to confirm if their guess is correct.

11 When a group has finished with one set they exchange sets with a different group. The activity ends when the groups have dealt with all the words in all the sets.

SAMPLE PRODUCT	WORD	CATEGORY
	operate	verb
	operating	gerund
	operation	noun
	operator	noun person
	operative	adjective
	operable	adjective: 'can be operated'
	cooperation	abstract noun: 'operating together'
	cooperative	adjective: 'operating together'
	cooperatively	adverb: 'together'
	inoperative	adjective, neg. prefix
	inoperable	adjective, neg. prefix: 'cannot be operated'

VARIATION 1

When doing stage 10, students in each group can score points for each word they guess correctly.

VARIATION 2

If there are particular families you would like to work on with your students, you can assign words to each group in stage 1, instead of letting them choose.

VARIATION 3

Groups write only the words from the families on pieces of paper, without the categories. They exchange their sets with other groups. Elicit the names of the grammatical categories from the class and write these as headings horizontally at the top of the board. Groups look at their sets of words and stick or write the words on the board under the appropriate heading. When they have finished, the whole class checks whether all the words are in the right columns.

REMARKS   **1** In stage 2 the definitions may sometimes need to be very detailed. For example, if the students choose the word *execute*, they must distinguish between *executor, executioner,* and *executive.*

2 In stage 8, by checking their own set of words, students remind themselves of the grammatical categories and check that the exercise can be done.

3 This is a good activity for making students aware of the word-building process and reminding them of grammatical categories. In word-building tests they often forget about the differences between adjectives and adverbs, or about negatives. This activity sensitizes them to these problems.

8 How to think learner-based teaching

Introduction

This book is a collection of activities which we have designed for our purposes, to meet the demands of our students and our syllabus. You may be asking yourself the question 'What am I to do if my teaching situation, goals, or learners are different?' Or you may be saying 'This is nothing new, I have already been doing some learner-based teaching in my lessons'.

In this section of the book we want to address these points and raise other questions. There is a saying: 'Give people a fish and you feed them for a day; teach them to fish and you feed them for life'. The activities we have presented were the 'fish'. Now we would like to consider the art of 'fishing'. We hope it will help you in developing your own independent learner-based teaching attitudes and thinking.

This section is divided into three parts. In the first we ask you to do an activity, rather like those the learners do, to encourage you to ask yourself some more questions, to think about how you already use the potential of your learners, and how you could use it more.

In the second part we present two activities to show in detail how lessons can be planned on the principles of such teaching.

In the third part we will suggest stages for introducing learner-based teaching into your repertoire.

How much learner-based teaching is there already in your teaching?

It may be worth reflecting on how much your learners already contribute to the lessons and how this contribution could be increased. We invite you to try the following activity, either alone or with some colleagues.

.

8.1 Teacher-based learning

LEVEL   **All levels**

TIME   **As much as you can spare**

PROCEDURE   1 Take a piece of paper. Fold it in two vertically and write on one side the heading 'materials' and on the other the heading 'activities'.

2 Recall your last three lessons.

3 Write on the piece of paper the materials you used from the coursebook or other sources, such as visuals, texts, and tapes.

4 Look at the materials and decide which of them could have been prepared by the students. How could you encourage them to prepare the materials?

5 Write on the other side of the piece of paper what the students did, for example played a game, read a text, did a grammar exercise.

6 Look at the activities and consider which could have been done by the students using materials produced in class.

7 Decide how to get the students to produce the material.

8 Decide what further activities can be based on the material produced by the students.

9 Calculate the time you spent on the preparation of the materials you used, for example, looking for pictures, writing and typing comprehension questions, recording programmes, studying the teacher's book, browsing through grammar books to find a suitable exercise, preparing role cards, photocopying.

10 Compare how much lesson time was involved in using the material and how effectively it was used. Was your preparation time worth it? Was the input proportional to the outcome of the lesson?

11 Last but not least, was the lesson enjoyable and unpredictable for both you and the learners?

REMARKS   1 By doing this activity you may have realized that there is already a significant element of learner-based teaching in your classroom.

2 You may also have realized that it is easy to expand the role of learner-based teaching in your lessons.

3 You may conclude that there are some activities that do *not* lend themselves to this approach in your teaching situation.

4 You may already be in a position to say how much learner-based teaching you can have or want in your lessons.

How to plan a learner-based lesson or activity

8.2 Planning a lesson: 1

PROCEDURE

1 Decide what the focus of the lesson is going to be, for example, giving directions.

2 Decide what materials are required, for instance a map.

3 Decide how to get the students to prepare a map. For example, students working in small groups could draw a map of a place with which they are all familiar. It may be best if the map includes where they are at the moment. Alternatively the class as a whole can prepare the map on the board.

4 Decide if any preparatory work is needed first, such as an activity where students recall the names of typical landmarks or orientation points such as the Post Office or Joe's Bistro. These should be real places that exist in the area they know and will appear in the map they will later draw.

5 If you decide such preparation is necessary, how do you organize it?

6 Decide how you want the students to use the map to practise giving directions. Will it be a written task or an oral task? Will they have the map in front of them or will they have to remember it? How can you structure the task so that students know they have performed it successfully? Will students themselves decide on a starting point or will one be given?

7 Decide whether you are going to give any language input, and if so, when? As they perform the task, earlier, or later (depending on how they do the task)?

REMARKS

1 There are a number of decisions you have to make in planning the lesson: about materials to be produced, classroom interaction, and so on. The sequence in which the decisions are given above does not necessarily reflect the sequence of stages in the lesson. For example, the decision in stage 4 actually concerns an activity which would precede the activity referred to in stage 3.

2 As students are drawing the map, they will be asking each other and you for words in English. They are reconstructing a real map and at the same time learning the English words needed to describe their own reality. They are not learning the words in connection with a totally unknown or non-existent place.

3 If you want to give language input as learners do the task, it may be better to make this a written task, so that *they* have the time to ask you how to say things and *you* have the time to answer and make sure they write it down accurately.

4 In stage 7 you may decide to let learners complete the activity, but note down what difficulties they had and come back to it in a subsequent lesson. In this case the activity serves as needs analysis, giving you the opportunity to see exactly where this group of learners has problems.

8.3 Planning a lesson: 2

PROCEDURE

1 Decide on the lesson focus, for example revising future tenses.

2 Decide what materials might be useful, for example horoscopes perhaps, for this activity.

3 Decide what you want the students to do in the lesson: talk, read, or write about the future with genuine interest.

4 Decide how to organize the activity so that the learners are involved in both preparing material and practising the focus area. How can the activities be integrated, so that the learners have a genuine interest in what they will read and a reason for talking about it afterwards?

5 Decide whether you want the students to read texts, i.e. horoscopes, that are grammatically correct. This will affect how the activity is structured and conducted.

6 Decide whether you are going to provide language input while the activity is in progress, or use the activity as a needs analysis exercise to reveal exactly where there are problems or gaps that need further attention, or do both.

SAMPLE PRODUCT

This is one way an activity could be structured, based on the above decisions.

1 Ask the students to shout out times or dates in the future, for example *in five minutes, this time next year, in July 2013, next Thursday*. Write all of these on the board.

2 Pair students off.

3 They tell each other about their lives at the moment, for example, where they live, what they do, their marital status, and their current interests, etc.

4 Individually, learners write horoscopes for their partners based on what their partners have just told them and incorporating the random dates on the board.

5 As they are writing help them with any language problems.

6 When they have finished they go back to their partners, exchange horoscopes, and read what has been predicted for them.

7 In their pairs learners comment on the predictions, whether they consider them likely or impossible, and on the language used.

VARIATION

If teachers want students to read texts that are absolutely correct they can plan the activity so that learners write the horoscopes in the first lesson. They can then be checked before the next lesson.

REMARKS

1 In this suggested activity the learners have produced horoscopes based on the information they received from their partners, who are therefore genuinely interested in reading the texts. There is also a genuine reason to talk about what they have read.

2 In stage 5 the teacher is helping with problems and providing language input on request. It is unlikely that there would be enough time in class to ensure that the finished horoscopes are absolutely correct. This is why in stage 7 there is an element of peer correction (but see Variation 1 above). This stage also serves as needs analysis, showing the teacher what needs further work in subsequent lessons.

3 All the informational input comes from the students: the dates, the personal information, and the finished horoscopes.

4 There are elements of surprise in this activity: for example, in stage 2/3 there is a switch from the future dates of stage 1 back to the present, and learners cannot be sure of what will happen next.

Introducing learner-based teaching into your classroom

Having used some of the activities in this book and worked through the activity in 8.1 above, you may have discovered that there is already an element of learner-based teaching work in your teaching. The first stage is to become aware of how much you are already doing and consider how you can expand it. You may, however, still feel apprehensive about preparing your own activities. It may help to do this progressively.

You might start by taking familiar material into the classroom, for example a text from the coursebook, and replacing one of the activities on the text with learner-based activities. As a second step you might choose to use a short, self-contained activity as part of a longer lesson. It is not necessary to start off with activities that last the entire lesson.

If you find that the activities are working and your confidence is increasing, you can then introduce longer ones which will take up more and more lesson time. This might lead you to try basing an entire lesson on a learner-based activity. You may then find that more and more of your lessons can be completely learner-based. As a further step, if you are teaching on a short course you could consider whether the entire programme can be learner-based.

Other titles in the Resource Books for Teachers series

CALL, by David Hardisty and Scott Windeatt – offers the teacher a bank of practical activities, based on communicative methodology, which make use of a variety of computer programs. (ISBN 0 19 437105 0)

Class Readers, by Jean Greenwood – is a comprehensive collection of activities offering practical advice and suggestions on how to exploit class readers to promote language and to develop both perceptive and literary skills. (ISBN 0 19 437103 4)

Classroom Dynamics, by Jill Hadfield – a practical book designed to help teachers establish and maintain a good working relationship with their classes, and so promote effective learning. It contains activities for ice-breaking, fostering self-confidence and group identity, and the end of term, plus a chapter on 'coping with crisis'. (ISBN 0 19 437147 6)

Conversation, by Rob Nolasco and Lois Arthur – the authors' approach is to examine what native speakers do when they 'make conversation', and then to use this information as the basis for more than eighty activities. (ISBN 0 19 437096 8)

Drama, by Charlyn Wessels – used effectively, drama can change a roomful of strangers into a happy cohesive group and make the process of language learning a great deal more creative and enjoyable. (ISBN 0 19 437097 6)

Grammar Dictation, by Ruth Wajnryb – offers an innovative approach to the study of grammar in the language classroom. The procedure (sometimes called 'dictogloss') encourages student reconstruction of texts. (ISBN 0 19 437004 6)

Literature, by Alan Maley and Alan Duff – is not a book on how to study literature, but on how to use it for language practice. The activities described can be used not only with the sample material provided, but also with other materials of the teacher's own choice. (ISBN 0 19 437094 1)

Music and Song, by Tim Murphey – contains ideas for using all types of music and song in the classroom in lively and interesting ways. It shows teachers how 'tuning in' to their students' musical tastes can increase motivation and tap a rich vein of resources. (ISBN 0 19 437055 0)

Newspapers, by Peter Grundy – champions a different approach from the usual use of newspapers for comprehension. Its aim is to give students the confidence to buy and read English-language newspapers for themselves, by first demystifying them, then looking at layout, use of pictures, and personal responses to stories. (ISBN 0 19 437192 1)

Project Work, by Diana L. Fried-Booth – a collection of full-scale projects of different kinds, lengths, and complexity is described in detail. The activities involved bridge the gap between the classroom and the outside world. (ISBN 0 19 437092 5)

Role Play, by Gillian Porter Ladousse – encompasses an extremely varied collection of activities ranging from highly controlled conversations to improvised drama, and from simple dialogues to complex scenarios. (ISBN 0 19 437095 X)

Self-Access, by Susan Sheerin – is designed to help EFL and ESL teachers with the practicalities of setting up and managing self-access study facilities and so enable learning to take place independently of teaching. (ISBN 0 19 437099 2)

Translation, by Alan Duff – explores the role of translation in language learning and provides the teacher with a wide variety of translation activities from many different subject areas. No specialist knowledge or previous experience of translation is required. (ISBN 0 19 437104 2)

Video, by Richard Cooper, Mike Lavery, and Mario Rinvolucri – differs radically from other books on this topic in that it encourages students to control the interaction between camera and image, thus providing a wide range of communicative situations and activities.

Vocabulary, by John Morgan and Mario Rinvolucri – emphasizes activities which encourage the students' own personal response, while facilitating exploration and extension of the language. This book will be of use to all teachers, including those in non-EFL classrooms. (ISBN 0 19 437091 7)

Writing, by Tricia Hedge – presents a range of writing tasks within a framework of current thinking on the process of writing. It discusses the different areas of writing ability and looks at ways in which classroom activities can help learners to develop these skills. (ISBN 0 19 437098 4)